D1347224

CAREERS FOR

SELF-
STARTERS

& Other Entrepreneurial Types

WESTMEATH LIBRARY
WITHDRAWN STOCK

VGM Careers for You Series

CAREERS FOR

SELF-
STARTERS

& Other Entrepreneurial Types

BLYTHE CAMENSON

SECOND EDITION

VGM Career Books

New York   Chicago   San Francisco   Lisbon   London   Madrid   Mexico City
Milan   New Delhi   San Juan   Seoul   Singapore   Sydney   Toronto

Library of Congress Cataloging-in-Publication Data

Camenson, Blythe
  Careers for self-starters & other entrepreneurial types / Blythe Camenson —
2nd ed.
      p.   cm. — (VGM careers for you series)
    ISBN 0-07-143728-2 (alk. paper)
      1. New business enterprises—Management.   2. Small business—
  Management.   3. Self-employed.   I. Title: Careers for self-starters and
  other entrepreneurial types.   II. Title.   III. Series.

  HD62.5.C35   2004
  658'.041—dc22   2004004107

Copyright © 2005 by The McGraw-Hill Companies, Inc. All rights reserved. Printed in
the United States of America. Except as permitted under the United States Copyright
Act of 1976, no part of this publication may be reproduced or distributed in any
form or by any means, or stored in a database or retrieval system, without the prior
written permission of the publisher.

1 2 3 4 5 6 7 8 9 0   DOC/DOC   3 2 1 0 9 8 7 6 5 4

ISBN 0-07-143728-2

McGraw-Hill books are available at special quantity discounts to use as premiums
and sales promotions, or for use in corporate training programs. For more
information, please write to the Director of Special Sales, Professional Publishing,
McGraw-Hill, Two Penn Plaza, New York, NY 10121-2298. Or contact your local
bookstore.

873,472 / 658 · 041

WESTMEATH COUNTY LIBRARY

This book is printed on acid-free paper.

*To Marshall Cook, who knows how to
get me started and keep me going*

Contents

Acknowledgments

The author would like to thank the following self-starters for providing information about their careers:

Jim Anderson, stained-glass artist, Anderson Glass Arts, Boston, Massachusetts

Tom Bernardin, author and self-publisher, *The Ellis Island Immigrant Cookbook,* New York, New York

Matthew Carone, owner, Carone Gallery, Fort Lauderdale, Florida

Dana Cassell, founder, Cassell Network of Writers, North Stratford, New Hampshire

Frank Cassisa, certified personal trainer, Boca Raton, Florida

Tom Doyle, owner, Palmetto Carriage Works, Charleston, South Carolina

Connie and Jeffrey Gay, producers, MurderWatch Mystery Theater, Orlando, Florida

Bob Haehle, freelance garden writer, Fort Lauderdale, Florida

Steve Herrell, owner, Herrell's Ice Cream, Northampton, Massachusetts

David Hirsch, chef and author, Moosewood Restaurant, Ithaca, New York

Way Hoyt, arborist, Tree Trimmers and Associates, Fort Lauderdale, Florida

David Kaufelt, founder, Key West Walking Tour, Key West, Florida

Robin Landry, esthetician, Coral Springs, Florida

Al Mendoza, owner, Keepsake Flowers and Gifts, Dolton, Illinois

Joe Nickell, paranormal investigator, Committee for the Scientific Investigation of Claims of the Paranormal (CSICOP), Center for Inquiry, Amherst, New York

Adam Perl, owner, Pastimes, Ithaca, New York

Mary Ptak, owner, The Stock Exchange, Fort Lauderdale, Florida

Jim Ridolfi, auctioneer, Aspon Trading Company, Troy, Pennsylvania

Adriana and Rick Rogers, owners, Grace Bentley Theatrical Productions, Carmel, New York

Roger and Mary Schmidt, owners and innkeepers, 18 Gardner Street Inn, Nantucket, Massachusetts

Rosalind Sedacca, advertising copywriter, Rosalind Sedacca and Associates, Vero Beach, Florida

Michael Silvestri, hair stylist/salon owner, Hollywood, Florida

Carol Stull, grower, CRS Growers, Finger Lakes Organic Growers Cooperative, Ithaca, New York

Joyce Sweeney, young adult writer, Coral Springs, Florida

Nancy Yost, literary agent, partner, Lowenstein-Yost Associates, New York, New York

CHAPTER ONE

Opportunities for Self-Starters

Many people dream of being their own boss, of finding endeavors that will let them work for themselves. They fantasize about any number of enterprises: converting an old home to an inn or bed-and-breakfast, collecting antiques and opening a shop in which to sell them, working in their own artist's studio, putting a green thumb to use in their own floral shop or nursery, opening a restaurant, or writing a book and seeing it published.

Self-starters go beyond dreaming. They plan a business or project, implement those plans, and, if all goes well, reap the benefits. How do they do it? There's no set formula for success, but self-starters share many of the same characteristics and take many of the same steps to get their enterprises off the ground.

In *Careers for Self-Starters* you will meet two dozen entrepreneurs, people who had a dream and made it come true. You will learn how each self-starter got going, obtained the necessary expertise, acquired financing, and made his or her business succeed. You will hear what pitfalls to avoid, and you'll come away with some sound advice for proceeding in similar enterprises.

Most importantly, *Careers for Self-Starters* is a book about ideas. You will learn about some traditional enterprises, some not-so-traditional ones, and some you might never have thought of. The ideas within these pages will spark other ideas or inspire spinoffs and twists on tried-and-true ones.

But first, let's see if you've got what it takes.

Self-Starter or Dreamer?

Dreamers are creative, imaginative, and innovative people. They fantasize about what could be, perhaps indulging in utopian visions of the perfect dream quest. They are romantics, idealists, and often delightful companions and friends. But unless they possess a few additional qualities, dreamers they will stay.

Self-starters dream. They're imaginative and creative, too. But they are also go-getters—independent individuals ready to turn their dreams into reality. They're willing to take risks and are not afraid to blaze their own trails. Some are even mavericks, standing out from the crowd, carving out unique niches for themselves.

Take this short true-false quiz and see if you relate to the traits typical of dreamers or self-starters.

1. I've lived in various cities, even traveled or worked abroad.
2. It's easy for me to pick up the phone and call someone I don't know.
3. If I were my own boss, I could work only three or four days a week if I wanted to.
4. I have a sound source of financing and won't have to worry about expenses for the first year or two.
5. I expect to get rich beyond my wildest dreams.
6. I never plan ahead. I prefer to be spontaneous.
7. I'm always late, I can never find my keys, and I sure could use a good secretary to keep me organized.
8. Tax forms and spreadsheets scare the pants off me, but I muddle through.
9. I leave computers to the other guys.
10. Good contacts and luck are all it takes. I have a spot on the fast track.

Let's tally up. See how often your answers match the ideal responses for self-starters, as follows:

1. **True.** Packing up and moving to a new place takes a certain kind of courage, not unlike that involved with starting a new business.
2. **True.** Entrepreneurs often have to make a lot of cold calls for publicity, information, and myriad other reasons.
3. **False.** Independent business owners usually work more hours than the average person employed by someone else. Seven-day work weeks are not unusual; for some, they're the norm.
4. **True.** A new business can take anywhere from one to five years to start showing a profit. It's important to have a source of income to take care of expenses during that time.
5. **False.** Although you might become rich—some do—starting out with that expectation is setting yourself up for disappointment or even failure.
6. **False.** Starting a new venture and keeping it going takes lots of planning. If you don't plan, it's like taking a trip without a road map. How will you end up where you hope to be, if you don't even know where you're going?
7. **False.** Good secretaries are expensive to hire. Most new entrepreneurs find they must wear a lot of different hats. Organizational skills are very important. Being a good juggler helps, too.
8. **False.** A solid business background is crucial to the success of any enterprise. Muddling through won't cut it.
9. **False.** Being computer literate is absolutely essential in this day and age.
10. **False.** By now you've probably figured out that luck, although occasionally coming into play for the . . . well, the lucky ones . . . has little to do with success.

How did you do? A total of 80 to 100 percent marks you as a self-starter. Anything below, and you're still dreaming! In any event, read on. All self-starters began as dreamers.

The Finances Involved

Do you need to be rich to start your own business? It certainly helps. But although several of the enterprises profiled in the pages to come required substantial backing to get off the ground, others were started on a shoestring.

It's nice to have a fat bank account but more important to have a good credit history—or a rich uncle. See how others managed it; it might help you figure out what to do.

Ideas, Ideas, Ideas

You're probably a first-time entrepreneur itching to go out on your own. You have some capital behind you, some business know-how, and the whole world out there to conquer. But what kind of enterprise should you venture into? That depends, of course, on your interests, skills, and prior experience. Let's have a look at what's to come and see what ideas it might ignite for you.

Dream Schemes

Who hasn't dreamed of opening a bed-and-breakfast or creating a national fad? We'll meet the operator of a historic inn on Nantucket Island, a man who thinks buses and cars are old-fashioned, another man who knows how to express any emotion with flowers, and a man who wanted to re-create a childhood experience producing homemade ice cream.

Artistic Visions

Self-starters with artistic talent or an eye for the value of an object will find someone in this section to inspire their dreams. Here you will read about an acclaimed stained-glass artist, the owner of a successful art gallery, a couple of collectors who know how to buy and sell their wares, and the people who evaluate and sell merchandise.

Service Industry Careers

In today's economy, service businesses are more and more the way to go. Offer to do something for other people or companies that they can't do for themselves, and you'll find scores of avenues to pursue. It's a broad highway, covering everything from hair care, personal training, and tracing family histories to plant sitting and tree trimming. You'll get some ideas from Chapter 4, then you can narrow down the field for yourself.

Careers in the Limelight

If you're comfortable performing in front of others, if public speaking comes naturally to you, and if you thrive on the response of a receptive audience, then here's where you'll find a few ideas to put you on the stage—so to speak.

Freelance Writing

Ah, the writer's life—being your own boss, working at home, setting your own hours. From freelancer to novelist to literary agent, learn about the different writing fields you can enter and how to go about making a success of them.

Organizations and Cooperative Enterprises

Dreamers hope to find a club or organization to join that matches their interests; self-starters see the need and start their own. Learn how a successful collective is started, how to form an association or organize a seminar business—all careers for highly organized individuals.

There are literally thousands and thousands of ideas for self-starter careers. Just look around you: every Wendy's, every Kinko's, every Sam's Club or Costco, every boutique or bookstore was started by someone with a dream. Think back to hula hoops and the happy face. These, too, were started by dreamers who weren't afraid to move on to self-starter status. Certainly there's room for one more Rubik's cube, one more published book, one more chocolate chip cookie stand. You too can join the ranks of successful entrepreneurs—all you have to do is stop dreaming and start moving.

For More Information

In addition to all the profiles and career details contained within each chapter, you'll find information on related professional associations in Appendix A. Recommended readings for various career areas are listed in Appendix B.

CHAPTER TWO

Dream Schemes

Many people hold the same dream—to become self-employed. They also share many of the same dreams about how to do so. Operating a bed-and-breakfast, a florist shop, or a specialty store are just a few of the popular ventures self-starters choose to pursue.

For some, these dreams are made into reality for a first career; for others, they offer a second career to look forward to, perhaps later in life, during retirement years.

Read on to see how others have fulfilled their dreams.

Operating Your Own Bed-and-Breakfast

Many entrepreneurs have been caught up in a movement popular throughout the country—restoring and refurbishing historic homes and converting them into country inns, guest houses, and bed-and-breakfast establishments.

Nantucket Island, just thirty miles off the coast of Massachusetts, is a showcase for these houses. Many of them are original Quaker homes, simple but sturdy dwellings, and perfectly preserved Georgian, Federal, and Greek Revival houses. Some of them are impressive mansions, the legacy of the wealth-producing whaling industry. Others are small, dollhouse-like affairs with geranium-filled planter boxes beneath lace-curtained, leaded-glass windows.

A glimpse inside any of these homes reveals various old-world antiques, such as carved mahogany sea chests and sleigh-back or canopied beds, many with shiny brass or even solid silver fixtures. White wicker rockers grace wooden porches, and widow's walks curve around under cedar-shake roof shingles.

Tourism supports the seven thousand or so year-round residents (the summer population blossoms to nearly fifty thousand each year), but the Nantucket Historical Association has a strong influence, and residents enthusiastically adhere to strict building codes. Although lines of fast-food stands and high-rise hotels often mar other tourist spots, no intrusive golden arches or glaring neon signs are allowed on the island. Even the gas stations are disguised, their red-brick structures blending perfectly with their surroundings.

Roger and Mary Schmidt, Innkeepers

Roger and Mary Schmidt own an inn, called simply the 18 Gardner Street Inn, on Nantucket Island. The Colonial-style house, which is on the historical walking tour, was built in 1835 by Captain Robert Joy. The sea captain took the proceeds of his last whaling excursion and built the house to retire in. Over the years, the house was owned by several families. In the 1940s the property was converted to a lodging house with six or seven rooms. The next family that purchased the inn installed bathrooms in the rooms and ran it as a bed-and-breakfast.

The Schmidts acquired the inn in 1988. The building is a traditional square box shape with a pitched roof and an ell in the back where the kitchen was added in the late 1800s. In front there's a center door with original hand-rolled glass windows on each side. A typical Nantucket friendship staircase graces the front door, with steps on either side meeting at the landing at the top. Weathered cedar shakes (which, along with the famous Nantucket fog, help to contribute to the island's other nickname, the "Gray Lady") and a large widow's walk complete the picture of an elegant sea captain's mansion.

Spread throughout the inn's two stories and finished third-floor attic are twelve guest rooms furnished with pencil-post, canopied, and four-poster beds, as well as antique mahogany or cherry dressers and nightstands. All of the rooms are airy; many are spacious suites, most with working fireplaces.

Roger, Mary, and their two children occupy a two-bedroom apartment in the finished basement. During the first two years they owned the inn, the Schmidts completely refurnished it. In the third and fourth years, they began a massive restoration of the guest rooms. They took all the wallpaper down and repaired dozens of cracks they discovered in the plaster. They upgraded the bathrooms and, keeping the period appearance of the bedrooms, repapered with pastels and satin wall coverings. They completely gutted the kitchen and replaced it with a new commercial kitchen so they could serve guests a full breakfast. And, as so often happens in old houses, they discovered a beautiful fireplace hidden for years behind one of the plaster walls. Every three years or so, the exterior of the house gets a new paint job.

One thing the Schmidts avoided was putting up new walls. They specifically chose an inn that wouldn't require extensive reconstruction work. They learned from experience that putting up drywall can be unbelievably expensive and complicated, and the same is true for dealing with commercial building codes. Because their property had been licensed for so many years as an inn, the Schmidts didn't have to be relicensed, although they do have to renew their license annually through the local building inspector.

How the Schmidts Got Started

The Schmidts are originally from Springfield in western Massachusetts. They honeymooned on Nantucket in 1977 and fell in love with the island. They started visiting three and four times a year. But when they began searching for property to buy, it became obvious that the selling prices were way out of their reach.

Roger explains: "In the early eighties, property on Nantucket skyrocketed. I was in the electronics field, Mary worked in a photography lab, and the dream of owning a summer home got pushed aside because of economics. We went to the nearby island of Martha's Vineyard because we'd heard there were good buys there. We ended up finding some property there and got into the real estate business. We bought a mariner's home and completely restored it and turned it into a small, five-bedroom inn. We developed some other pieces of property there as well. This was all happening while we were still considering Springfield as our main residence. Eventually we sold it all off and came back to Nantucket in a much better financial condition to buy our current property."

Avoiding the Pitfalls

For the first two years, the Schmidts hired an innkeeper to run 18 Gardner Street. Unfortunately, they nearly went bankrupt due to mismanagement, so in 1990 the family moved to the island permanently and started running the inn themselves. As Roger describes it, "Business took off like a cannonball."

Roger Schmidt is realistic about how hard it can be to make a success of a business like his. He cautions that "anybody who gets into this business and thinks he or she will succeed by serving the greatest cup of coffee and greeting every guest with a warm smile is totally wrong. It's not enough." Roger stresses the importance of good advertising for a business like his, where prospective customers cannot actually see what they will be getting for their money. The Schmidts use major newspapers such as the *Boston Globe* and the *New York Times*, and the inn is listed on several Internet travel sites.

Once the guests do arrive, the Schmidts must anticipate their needs and strive to accommodate them in order to keep repeat business and word-of-mouth advertising alive. By paying close attention, the Schmidts realized that their guests found it inconvenient to walk to town to get rented bicycles, so they purchased bicycles that they provide free to guests. They also gathered that guests would like more than a continental breakfast, so they obtained a food-service permit and now offer a full breakfast every day. They provide dockside shuttle service from the ferry, picnic baskets, beach blankets, and ice coolers. Keeping the fire-places in working order to warm guests after a cold autumn walk from town keeps the fall business alive.

Roger sums it up this way: "A lot of people want to live out their romantic dream by retiring to an idyllic spot such as Nantucket and running a bed-and-breakfast. But the first major mistake they make is when they use the word 'retiring.' There's nothing retiring, or romantic, about operating an inn. You have to work very hard.

"From April 1 to November 31, my day is primarily involved with taking reservations, handling problems, and delegating responsibilities to our staff of five. During the winter, we involve ourselves with marketing, and interior design and restoration. We're always busy."

The Finances Involved

Roger and Mary Schmidt paid $850,000 for 18 Gardner Street in 1988. At that time, this was a very good price. Over the next two years the property value dropped to $600,000, but due to the ren-ovations and the steady clientele, the property and business are now worth over $1 million.

The bed-and-breakfast is open year-round, with nightly rates ranging from $150 to $350 during the high season. Monthly oper-ating expenses and mortgage payments are very high also.

Roger says, "Nantucket, of course, is a small and very expensive island. There are many areas in the country where you could pick up a small house or an established inn for around $100,000.

"Whatever the value, the trick is to have an understanding of real estate financing and to try to be a little creative. In our case, we put very little down; the owner was willing to hold back a sec-ond mortgage. Another alternative is to lease with an option to buy. We've just done that with the property adjoining ours, and now we have five more guest rooms to book.

"But I would advise starting out with a property with just three or four guest rooms. It's a very risky business, and there's a high burnout and turnover rate. Sometimes the dream can turn into a nightmare. You can't treat it as a dream. You have to treat it as a business."

Tom Doyle, Carriage Tour Operator

"There's nothing better than a good mule; there's nothing worse than a bad one," says Tom Doyle, owner of the Palmetto Carriage Works, a horse- and mule-drawn carriage tour company in Charleston, South Carolina. "The thing about the bad ones, though, is that they don't hide it very well. I can spend an afternoon with a mule and know whether or not it's going to work. A horse will go by something ninety-nine times as if it wasn't there, but on the hundredth time, the time you're not paying attention, the horse will absolutely freak out. Mules are much easier to train."

And if anyone should know the characteristics of mules, it's Tom Doyle. He has built up his tour business over three decades and now employs twenty-eight people, owns a stable right in the heart of the city, and has twenty-six carriages, two horses, and twenty-eight mules.

"The fellow who began the business started off with just the frame of an old farm wagon," says Tom. "He built some seats and a roof on top of it. He also had a carriage from the Jack Daniel's Brewery, and he picked up a few old carriages from auctions. But they're not really built heavy-duty enough for the kind of work we use them for, and they're too small. It's hard to find an antique carriage that will carry six or sixteen people. Because of that, we began designing our own carriages."

Tom employs one person who does nothing but build carriages. He also has a full barn staff, an office manager, a bookkeeper, a secretary, a ticket collector, and drivers who double as grooms. But everyone is also a licensed tour guide. "The key to doing well in the carriage business," Tom explains, "is when the business is here, you've got to be able to handle it, and when it's not here, you have to be able to get real small. We're very seasonal."

How Tom Got Started

Tom Doyle came to Charleston from New Jersey to study at the Citadel. When he finished with his B.A. in history, he looked around for work he would enjoy. But most of the things he liked to do didn't pay enough money to support a family, so he was often forced to hold two jobs. It was through this moonlighting that he discovered the Palmetto Carriage Works, starting as a part-time carriage driver–cum–tour guide. Within a year, Tom had graduated to full-time driver and was working sixty to seventy hours a week. When the original owner decided it was time to retire in 1982, he offered the business to Tom. "I didn't have a dime at the time," Tom admits, "but he gave me such a good deal, I was able to go out and find some other people who were willing to invest, and I put together a little group of silent partners."

It's possible to start small in this business, Tom maintains. You don't need an office or a ticket collector or a fleet of carriages. With an investment of about $8,000 for the carriage, tack, animal, and various permits, you can position yourself in a place that's visible to tourists—outside a visitor's information center or a popular hotel or tourist attraction. "It's a see-and-do thing," says Tom. "The carriages themselves are the best advertising. Tourists will ask the driver, 'Hey, how do I get on one of these?'"

Making a Go of It

To make it work you have to live the business, Tom warns. You have to be out there driving every day, making friends, and getting to know everyone. Then word of mouth will get you going.

Tom also markets his business to big hotels and meeting planners and has found his niche with large groups. The Mills House Hotel and the Charleston Place Hotel, two of the city's premier accommodations, have chosen Palmetto Carriage Works to operate the carriages owned by the hotels.

Tom also offers two wedding packages for the bride and groom who want to be transported to their ceremony in old-fashioned style. Ranging from $150 to $275, the wedding packages include decorated carriages and appropriately attired drivers. The company also offers private carriage tours beginning at $75. The company's website, www.carriagetours.com, offers complete information about the tours, including a Letterman-style top ten list of why Palmetto Carriage Works is the best choice for touring Charleston.

Tom also runs a free shuttle service with his 1934 antique Ford bus. He moves his customers from the visitor's center to his starting point. "But the real bread and butter of the business is the walk-up tourist."

Tom's tours are an hour long and cover twenty blocks of the old city. Drivers provide a nonstop narration covering Charleston's history, architecture, gardens, people, and points of interest.

"As opposed to a motorized tour, our drivers can turn and talk to the people and make eye contact," Tom says. "It's a leisurely business. While you're waiting for the carriage to fill up, you chat with the passengers. To have a really great tour you need to get to know your customers. And tourists are great to deal with because 99.9 percent of them are in a good mood. They're on vacation, after all! When I take people on a carriage tour, everyone in the city benefits because I leave them so happy with Charleston, they're wanting to do more and to come back."

A Few Golden Rules

To have a successful tour business, you must love the city where you work, and you have to be an expert and know everything about its local history. "Good business sense is also important," Tom says. "And when you're the boss, you have to monitor your drivers—the tour they give is the most important part. I occasionally pay strangers to ride and check out the drivers."

Tom is convinced that running a successful tour company is more than a job; it's a lifestyle. "You get to work with the animals, which I really like; you can bring your children to work; all the neighborhood kids come around the stables to help out and get free rides. You have to do a good job. You're not only representing yourself, you're representing the whole city."

Where to Find That Carriage

Tom suggests finding an Amish settlement, where carriages and farm wagons are often for sale. There are large Amish communities in Pennsylvania, Indiana, Ohio, and Tennessee. Those states' departments of tourism can direct you to the settlements. The Internet is also a good source for finding carriages for sale.

Being a Florist

Florists either own and operate their own shops or work in shops for other people. There are three kinds of flower shops: cash-and-carry stores, decorator shops, and service shops.

Cash-and-carry stores, or merchandising stores as they are also known, sell bunches of prewrapped flowers. Generally, customers cannot order special arrangements through cash-and-carry shops; their selections are limited to what is immediately available and on hand. Cash-and-carry shops are found in the neighborhood supermarket, at farmers' markets, or at impromptu "shops" set up in buckets alongside the road.

Decorator shops, which are few and far between, operate as specialists, custom-making arrangements for important occasions such as weddings or balls. They generally do not cater to walk-in customers.

The highest percentage of florists are service florists, meaning they offer a service in addition to a product. They design, custom make, and deliver their merchandise.

Location, Location, Location

As with any business that hopes to garner off-the-street customers, location is always the first consideration. Because flowers are considered a luxury item rather than a necessity (although fervent plant lovers would surely argue), most successful florist shops are found in suburban town centers as opposed to downtown, inner-city locations. Florist shops also can do well in shopping malls.

The Skills You'll Need

To be a successful florist, a love of plants, although crucial, is not enough. Florists must have training in every aspect of the industry, including strong business skills. The best preparation is gaining a combination of on-the-job experience and education.

Trainees can gain experience working part-time for retail and wholesale florists, for greenhouses and nurseries, or for cut-flower growers. With this kind of exposure, potential florists can learn about packing and unpacking, processing, shipping, propagation, cutting, seed sowing, bulb planting and potting, the basics of floral design, and pickup, delivery, and sales work.

Students with dreams of owning florist shops should take courses in biological sciences, math, communications, computer science, and general business, including retail store management. Some academic and vocational institutions offer two- and four-year programs geared directly to floriculture and horticulture. Many also provide students with the opportunity for training while in school through cooperative education programs. Co-op programs place students in related business settings and, after the first year of academics, alternate semesters of work and study.

A number of colleges and post-secondary schools offer two- and four-year degree programs, and technical and certificate-awarding programs. The courses include general horticulture, ornamental horticulture, floriculture, and floral design. The Society of American Florists provides information on such programs; contact information for the society is given in Appendix A.

Al Mendoza is proprietor of Keepsake Flowers and Gifts in Dolton, Illinois. He is also assistant director at the American Floral

Art School in Chicago. Al says, "I always tell any student who is coming to our school and planning on opening up a flower shop that it's great to know floral design, but it's more important to have a business degree than a floral degree. More businesses fail because they think of it as an art business rather than an actual commercial business. If people want to get their training through college, they should major in business with a minor in floral design.

"I can take people off the street and teach them design," he continues. "It's very mechanical. You establish your height, your width, your depth. The art part is where the talent comes in."

Many floral designers and future florist shop owners get their training working in florist shops, learning as they go. They also attend seminars and workshops and take courses at floral design schools. The American Floral Art School, in business for more than fifty years, is one of the best known in the world. It offers an intensive three-week course, after which Al Mendoza says students will graduate as competent designers with a good understanding of the basics.

"A three-week course is enough to help a student get his or her foot in the door at a flower shop," Al explains. "But really, three weeks is not enough. The rest of the training comes from on-the-job experience. But it's a catch-22 situation. It's difficult to get that first job without some sort of training. Our program helps to open the door."

During the three-week program at the American Floral Art School, students study the art and mechanics of floral design. They learn the seven principles of floral design and how to apply them to everyday arrangements and specialty work. For additional training, students attend seminars and workshops sponsored by local wholesalers or the American Institute of Floral Designers (AIFD), which is the professional association to which floral designers strive to belong. Admission to this organization is very competitive.

The Downsides of the Job

Florists work long hours, and, as Al Mendoza says, "When most people are out enjoying the various parties, you're working at them. During holiday times, most people are having fun, enjoying the festivities, but again, it's the busiest time of the year for florists. In the floral world you don't get weekends and holidays off. I can't remember the last time my family and I could share a decent holiday together. Christmas, Easter . . . you're working like crazy the week before; then you're so exhausted, you can't enjoy yourself."

The Finances Involved

Starting a florist business requires an initial investment of about $100,000, and as with many small businesses, it can be several years before you see any real profit.

Al Mendoza says, "It's a risk when you're dealing with perishables. You can lose a lot if you don't know how to order. If you order too much you can lose, or if you don't order enough you can lose. A typical example would be Valentine's Day. If you order too many roses, if you buy a thousand too many, you can lose thousands of dollars. But it's hard to learn how to get the ordering right. That's why it's so important to work for other florists before venturing out on your own. You need the experience."

Food for Thought

In recent years, we have become nearly obsessed with food. Celebrity chefs appear on talk shows, entire television networks are dedicated to food, and a reality show detailed the opening of a new restaurant in New York City. It is not surprising, then, that many self-starters dream of opening a restaurant, café, coffee bar, or some other type of dining establishment. It's a risky business, anyone will tell you, and the trick is to find something new, a twist that will capture the attention of a large audience.

Just as coffee bars in New York City are the popular endeavor now, twenty-five years ago it was ice cream. Two decades ago, the first Steve's Ice Cream was a groundbreaker in a movement that brought people back to a more natural way of enjoying ice cream. Its founder, self-starter Steve Herrell, wanted to open a fun business, and he thought ice cream would be just the thing.

How Steve Got Started

"Ice cream has been around commercially for 140 years or so," says Steve, "and in the old days it was very good. But it started declining in quality, and around 1973 it had gotten about as low as it could get. At that time there seemed to be a sudden revelation that ice cream could be a lot better than what we'd been getting."

This was at the beginning of the public's interest in natural foods, vegetarian dining, and health food stores and restaurants. For Steve, the timing was right.

"I remembered our days at home when I was growing up, making ice cream in the backyard with the family. My dad and my great-uncle taught us all how to make it. We learned about the fun of everyone taking a turn at the crank, the anticipation when putting in the ice and salt, and the great moment when it was done and we opened it up and took out the dasher."

Steve Herrell is a certified high school English teacher in Massachusetts. After teaching for a while, he realized that the work was not to his liking, and he spent a couple of years earning a living by driving a taxi while he tried to decide what to do with his life. Steve knew that he wanted to own a business, and eventually ice cream seemed to be just the right thing.

Steve opened Steve's Ice Cream on Elm Street in Somerville, Massachusetts, on a Friday in June 1973. Within the first three days, he had a full crowd every night. He spent about $200 to advertise on WBCN, a popular radio station in Boston, but it was word of mouth that packed the place. The local press paid Steve's a lot of attention, and articles started appearing regularly in the *Boston Globe*. Not too much later came national recognition. The *New Yorker* magazine was the first: it showcased Steve's Ice Cream in its "Talk of the Town" section.

873.4721

WESTMEATH COUNTY LIBRARY

Steve's was the first parlor to make its own ice cream in full view of all the customers. Steve was also the first to popularize using "mix-ins," namely the crushed Heath bars, Oreo cookies, M&M's, and other goodies you can blend with your ice cream. Today using mix-ins is commonplace, but then it was pure novelty.

"I thought it would be a fun business," Steve explains, "an interesting thing to watch, making ice cream in full view on the premises. What this was was a business concept. I wanted it to be an active kind of a place, a place of function where something would be going on. We had a player piano, colorful pictures on the walls; there was a certain personal atmosphere to the place."

Interestingly, Steve feels that a certain lack of business savvy might actually have helped his business. As he says, "I earned a B.A. in sociology; I think, though, that if I had gone to business school and earned a business degree, I would not have done Steve's. Part of its attraction and charm was due to my obvious lack of business training. I was not following any kind of mold— it was a pure vision of what I thought it could be and how it should operate. If I had gone to business school, I might have been taught it wouldn't work."

The Finances Involved

"I started with almost nothing," Steve notes. "I used what personal savings I had and credit cards. It wasn't nearly enough, but because of that it was a very personal kind of place. For example, the chairs and tables didn't match. Normally, when opening a restaurant, you'd go out and buy twelve tables and chairs that were all the same. But I went to used furniture stores and picked out two chairs here, three there, and painted them orange, red, and purple. You wouldn't learn that in a business course.

"We sold out almost every night. I opened with just one or two employees, and I was making all of the ice cream and staying up every night to do it. I was very happy that it was so successful and so well received right away, but then I had to close for about two weeks to reorganize, to move in more equipment and hire more staff and train them to make ice cream. When I first opened, I didn't even have enough refrigeration space."

Usually with a new business you can't expect to break even or show a profit the first year or so, but that wasn't the case with Steve's. Steve made enough money to live on from the beginning, and the customers kept coming. In fact, he could have made even more. "The problem with Steve's was that the prices weren't high enough, so it always seemed as if there wasn't enough money. So I raised the prices and worried that the customers wouldn't want to come, but there was never any negative feedback. All through my four years there my prices could have been, should have been, at least 25 percent higher than they were."

The Formula for Success

Steve attributes his success to a variety of factors: "I never advertised that the ice cream was all natural, but people just picked that up and assumed it. My hope was to take cream and eggs and sugar and mix it up, flavor it, and freeze it. But health codes don't allow you to do just that in a retail situation. You need to use a prepackaged mixture made by a dairy processor under controlled conditions. It's homogenized and pasteurized—the pasteurization is an important part of the process. It doesn't have preservatives to make it last longer like you'd find in bread, for example, but it does have additives. The air content in my ice cream is very low, though, which means it tastes richer and you get more substance per teaspoon than in a high-air-content ice cream.

"Basically, the ice cream tastes great. I do my own flavoring, and that's all natural. I don't go for weird; I go for good. The flavors are unique, such as root beer or Earl Grey tea. Then there's malted vanilla, pure vanilla, pure chocolate, real strawberries.

"The idea of making the ice cream on the premises was unique; the mix-ins and the store itself all contributed to the success.

There was a real character to it. It wasn't a big impersonal chain then, and people could sense that there was a real person behind the whole thing. People related to that and liked it."

After Steve's

"I sold Steve's in August of 1977, all assets and liabilities," the entrepreneur explains. "There was a nice difference between my initial investment and the final sale price. The only thing I kept was the player piano."

Three partners bought Steve's and expanded it, then they sold it to a company called Integrated Resources, which then sold it to another partnership. Steve Herrell is not involved with any of the Steve's ice cream shops now located around the country.

Steve had a three-year noncompetition agreement with the people he sold to, and after it expired in August of 1980, he opened Herrell's Ice Cream in Northampton, Massachusetts.

Steve became interested in expanding and enlisted the services of a franchise consultant. He opened the first Herrell's franchise store in Harvard Square on Dunster Street in 1982. He says, "It's still there, and they use all my formulas and trademarks. At this time, there are two other franchises in Boston, as well as an ice cream bonbon plant."

Steve describes Herrell's as having "a very nonchain feel." He used the old player piano for a while, until the staff grew tired of hearing the same few songs played again and again by customers. "We have about twelve hundred square feet, decorated with Caribbean colors—greens and reds—a tin ceiling, and two giant stuffed bears sitting in the window having a dish of vanilla ice cream."

Steve has twenty-five employees, and he puts in about thirty-five hours a week at Herrell's. He could let employees handle the day-to-day tasks, but he still prefers to keep his hand in. "I could be semiretired now, but then I would start to lose touch with what's going on; you don't hear feedback from customers, and everything would be secondhand. I always appreciate it when customers come up and tell me how much they enjoy Herrell's, and lots of people come up to me who remember going to the Somerville store twenty years ago, standing in line, and having that unique ice cream experience."

Some Words of Advice

Steve says you should just go ahead and follow your vision—and don't go to business school. "I would have been more fearful if I had known what problems might have come up. If you get too much advice, you could be overwhelmed. I could make a list of all the potential problems and publish it, but it wouldn't be a good idea. Your creativity would get squelched."

To learn more about a different kind of restaurant success story, turn to Chapter 7.

CHAPTER THREE

Artistic Visions

Many who dream of being self-employed are artists who have natural talents that they hope to turn into viable careers. Others love collecting art or antiques and making them available to the public. Whether it's pottery or painting, sewing or stained glass, artistic self-starters can make a name for themselves and work full-time in their chosen areas. In this chapter we will meet entrepreneurs who have made their artistic dreams come true.

Jim Anderson, Stained-Glass Artist

Over the last twenty-five years, Jim Anderson has established himself as a successful stained-glass artist in Boston. His studio on Tremont Street in the revitalized South End neighborhood is called Anderson Glass Arts. Jim attended the School of the Museum of Fine Arts in Boston and the Massachusetts College of Art, graduating with a B.F.A. and a teaching certificate.

Jim's website, www.jimandersonstainedglass.com, describes him as "artist, craftsman, architect, and restorer." When did this renowned artist begin to create? "I started drawing and painting when I was young," says Jim. "Even in my baby book it says stuff like 'Jimmy is creative,' 'Jimmy is artistic,' 'Jimmy can draw.' It's one of the areas where I got affirmation as a child.

"I found that I really loved the combination of art and architecture, as opposed to paintings that just hang on walls. I liked the fact that stained glass becomes a permanent part of a building—it becomes architectural art."

Jim's designs include many styles, traditional as well as contemporary. He creates hand-painted glass like that seen in churches, as well as in styles from different periods, such as Victorian, Federal, and Edwardian.

How Jim Got Started

After finishing his bachelor of fine arts degree, Jim decided to pursue a teaching certificate as a way to guarantee an income if he could not support himself as an artist. But during that time, Jim realized that he actually was supporting himself. He started making windows for people, and it paid his way through school.

Jim recalls being fascinated by church windows as a child, and at age twenty-six he designed his first, for St. George's Greek Orthodox Church in Hyannis. In retrospect, Jim says, "Now I'm amazed at that kind of undertaking for such a young man. I remember that my colleagues in New York and other places were astounded that the commission for a church was given to such a young artist."

Jim says, "Commissions started coming because people saw the work I did on my own house. I own a brownstone in the South End, which is the largest Victorian neighborhood in America with more than two thousand structures intact—bowfronts and brownstones.

"I set up a workshop on the ground level of the townhouse so I'd have a place to work, then I did my doorways first. Other neighbors saw them and really loved them. Some of my neighbors were professional architects, and they asked if I'd do their doors. Then other people saw the work and it mushroomed. Over the years I've done ten or fifteen doors on my street alone, and then other people on different streets started seeing them and hiring me."

It wasn't long before an article about Jim's work appeared in the *Boston Globe*. Other papers followed suit, and a television documentary about revitalizing an old art form included Jim's work as well. Soon Jim was getting even more work, so he moved his studio out of his home to a more visible commercial area.

Jim now employs assistants to help him and to do repair and restoration work. Initially, the number of assistants depended on the economy and how much work Jim had. He would hire assistants when he had enough work but would have to let them go if things slowed down. As Jim's reputation has spread, however, he has a fully trained staff employed in his studio.

Jim describes his love for his work: "I like going to people's houses and making beautiful windows they really love and that I feel are appropriate for their homes. I wouldn't put a modern window in a Victorian, for example; it wouldn't be suitable.

"I meet a lot of interesting people in my work. Maybe it's because it's an unusual art form, and it's usually interesting people who want it. The work is fun and challenging, and I'm always learning something new. The older I get, the more complicated and sophisticated the commissions get."

The Finances Involved

"Money doesn't come in regularly, but it always seems to come in," says Jim, "sometimes in big chunks, sometimes in little chunks. I never know when or what, but I haven't starved, and I haven't not paid my bills yet."

Some Advice from Jim

"Follow your dream; listen to your gut on what to do. Visualize what you want for yourself, then slowly go toward it.

"But start slowly," he warns. "In my first studio, I made worktables out of plywood and other basic, simple things I could find. Nothing fancy or expensive—whatever I could scavenge. I've refined the space over time. Don't spend too much as you go along; let your business build up and don't overextend yourself.

"There are cooperative buildings for artists in lots of major cities now. It's nice to work around other artists and share old warehouse space. It gives you a lot of exposure, plus it keeps you in the art community, and the rents are usually reasonable.

"Just work hard and keep an eye on every aspect of the business, including the bookkeeping."

Matthew Carone, Gallery Owner

Matthew Carone is owner of the Carone Gallery, a prestigious establishment in Fort Lauderdale, Florida. He handles contemporary art—American, some European, and some Latin American paintings and sculpture. He is also an established painter himself and is often invited to show his work at other galleries.

The Carone Gallery, a family business, has been in existence since 1957. "I am the owner, and my wife is my partner," Matthew explains. "My son used to be an assistant director but left to work for our symphony here. Now I'm semiretired. I spend five months of the year in Lenox, Massachusetts, in the Tanglewood area where I have a studio, and the rest of the time is in Fort Lauderdale."

Matthew's schedule is made possible by the art season in South Florida. The winter months are the busiest, with the hot summers much slower in terms of sales. As he says, "During the summer months, if you're lucky, you just make ends meet. So we decided many years ago not to worry about the summers, to just relax. When people are back in the momentum of buying, we open our doors and everyone is clamoring to come in and see what's new for the year. So we close for five or six months of the year, and that works out well."

Matthew has a few ways of acquiring the art he exhibits. Since his gallery has an established reputation, there are several artists who want him to show their work. This allows him to be selective about what he acquires.

In the beginning, however, this luxury did not exist. As Matthew says, "When you're starting, you have to trust your taste and look for talent that may have yet to be discovered. Establish yourself as a serious gallery." In Matthew Carone's case, this happened with master graphics. He began acquiring original prints of Picasso, Cezanne, and Matisse and established a reputation as a gallery that dealt in serious works.

Starting Your Own Gallery

Matthew offers some advice for aspiring gallery owners. "First you decide what you want to sell and promote. Being idealistic about it is one way to go, if you have faith in a particular artist but you know his work would be difficult to sell. Great art is not always palatable on your initial response. Even Picasso, before he became famous, was laughed at by most of the people in the world. You have to be brave and have a conviction about the art, and that, of course, comes out of a love for it. You have to be sincere."

Once you have decided what type of art you want to acquire, you will need a place to exhibit it. Matthew emphasizes the importance of location, stating that proximity to a museum or other cultural area is ideal. While this might be expensive, it will ultimately be better than an inexpensive space in a less desirable location, and it will represent your largest expenditure.

"Think of the cost of a year's rent," Matthew says. "Other expenses are minimal. You have blank walls painted white, track lighting, a desk, and a little storeroom. There are advertising costs, brochures, announcements, your insurance and utilities, and any salaries you'll have to pay. That's the beginning. Then you have to get a stable of artists who would reflect your taste, who would help establish your image as a serious gallery."

There are, of course, different types of galleries. The owner of a craft gallery might see more financial success, since crafts are often more appealing—and affordable—to the public than fine art.

The Day-to-Day Running of an Art Gallery

"During a typical good day during the season—January, February, and March—I come in and put the coffee on, take a look at my show, and then, shortly thereafter, a client comes in and it becomes a social hour," Matthew explains. "We sit down and have a cup of coffee and she wants to see what we're showing. We get into dialogue and we're getting excited to the point where she says, 'I have to own it.' Or maybe not, or maybe something else. And that happens throughout the day.

"In addition to client contact, I talk with artists—artists who want to show with me. They send me slides, they want to see me, and I never refuse to talk to them. Part of the fun is looking at all the art and deciding who you want to show. The artist might be wonderful with beautiful art, but then you also have to evaluate whether or not you'll be able to sell it. Each space on the wall costs you X amount of money. You have to make your expenses, and every inch of wall space must try to pay for itself."

Matthew's day often includes talking with the artist whose work he is currently showing and making plans for the installation of any new shows. The art must be displayed so that each piece is seen to its best advantage, with decisions made about where each work belongs in relation to another piece. As Matthew explains it, "Hanging the art is something you need to have a feel for. It's very important to be able to hang an artist next to someone he's compatible with. You don't want any conflicts in image. You wouldn't want to put an ethereal kind of painting next to a very guttural abstract. You could destroy that very sensitive painting if it's within the view of something incompatible. You learn this on the job and through discussion, and it's a gut feeling. There's no one book that can describe this. There is a sense that one feels."

Matthew is always planning ahead, preparing for the next show. He usually shows an exhibit for three weeks, and then he takes a week off before the next show. In one season, he usually has four shows. After that, Matthew exhibits his own inventory of works that he owns.

"It's been the most wonderful life for me," Matthew states. "I can't tell you how great it's been. First of all, I'm a painter, I play the violin, and I use my gallery for concerts. I come to work thinking I'm coming home. I'm going to where I want to be. I love the artists, I love selling important stuff, I love people responding to my enthusiasm. It's been glorious. I'm a very lucky guy—I love what I do."

The Finances Involved

Most galleries work on a fifty-fifty basis with the artist. "But if it's a very popular artist," Matthew explains, "you might get only 30 percent. The cost of the artwork could range from $2,000 for a small wooden mask to $9,500 for paintings in the show I'm doing now. I've sold art for $43,000, and that's not the most expensive I've shown. With artists who have a following, the more popular they are, the bigger the attraction they are, the better for you."

Adam Perl, Antiques Dealer

"If you scratch a dealer, you'll find a collector underneath," reveals Adam Perl, proprietor of Pastimes, an antiques and collectibles shop in Ithaca, New York. "Many of us have gone into business just to finance our collecting habits."

Adam's own collecting habit began in the seventh grade when a classmate brought a book to school called *Cash for Your Coins*. But even if that hadn't happened, it's unlikely the collecting bug would have passed Adam by. He grew up surrounded by art and antiques; his mother is an art historian who worked at the Museum of Modern Art in New York, the Andrew Dickson White Museum at Cornell, and the Smithsonian's Hirshhorn Museum. His father was a writer, and both were serious antiques collectors.

Surprisingly, Adam had never been to an auction until he was a young adult. He had just rented an unfurnished apartment when he found out about a country auction being held nearby.

"I was instantly hooked. I spent $100 and filled my van three times. I furnished my entire apartment with items to spare. The early seventies was a golden age of buying, when wonderful three- and four-generation estates were being broken up all over the country, but especially in the Northeast. There wasn't much of an antiques market in any field then—you could buy anything for the proverbial song in those days."

With no thought of turning it into a business at that time, Adam began frequenting auctions for the fun of it. He'd go out with five or ten dollars in his pocket and come home with treasures. "I kept doing it over and over again, until I felt I had much more than I could fit in my apartment. I realized from seeing people's setups at flea markets that they had an organized system of pricing and that they generally specialized in a particular area, such as knives or dolls. I learned that if I took the things I bought and cleaned them up a bit—polished the brass, refinished the wood, and stove-blacked the iron—I could actually sell them for more than I had paid for them. I had my first garage sale and made a little money on it. It wasn't much of a step from that to connect with New York City and the contacts I had there."

How Adam Got Started

Adam talked to several dealers and tried to find people who were sympathetic to a novice and who were willing to teach him. At the time, though, the world of antiques was still a mystery, and few people would reveal their secrets or impart their knowledge to anyone else.

Adam found his sympathetic antiques dealers at American Hurrah, which is now a well-known New York City shop run by Joel and Kate Kopp, specializing in quilts and photographic images. "The Kopps were very forthcoming and didn't hold anything back. One thing they taught me is that you should try to double your money. You don't always do it, or sometimes you do better, but that's what you aim for. They taught me how to judge the condition of an item and how to develop and trust my own taste. They also helped to bail me out when I made mistakes."

Adam became a "picker," which is the industry term for a wholesaler. As Adam describes it, "The picker, during his antique-hunting expeditions, tries to pick out the one great item out of the ten thousand he sees. I would actually buy retail at shops in upstate New York, perhaps finding a quilt, beautifully made and in excellent condition, for twenty-five dollars to fifty dollars. I would take it to the city and sell it for double."

Based on advice from the Kopps, Adam began to look for fine cotton quilts hand-stitched in early nineteenth-century materials with good colors and patterns. He bought an unusual quilt at a garage sale for four dollars, even though it didn't meet those criteria. One of its most striking characteristics was that there was a man's wool tank-top bathing suit stitched right into it. Adam brought it to the Kopps in New York; they were kind enough to buy it for twelve dollars, even though they didn't think it was worth much. The Kopps later sold the quilt for fifty dollars, and after many more sales, it wound up in the Louvre Museum in Paris as an example of early twentieth-century American folk art. As Adam says, "Anybody who's been in business has made mistakes from time to time. Incidents like this can happen to the best of us."

Starting on a Shoestring

Adam opened his first shop in 1973 with just $400. An architect bought a condemned high school, then remodeled it and converted it into a lively arcade of shops and boutiques called the DeWitt Building.

Adam rented what he calls "an unpretentious hole-in-the-wall" for $125 a month. The landlord gave him some paint, and he bought a huge old machine-made oriental rug for one dollar. "The rug had several feet missing in the corner. I spent another dollar and bought a big overstuffed chair to cover the hole. After the $21 spent on decor, I had $148 left for merchandise."

Adam left the business for a few years and then returned in 1978 to open his current shop, Pastimes. "This is one of the best businesses to get into on little or no capital. You don't need any particular expertise or any particular degree. You do need to have some stock and a couple of tables and table coverings. And then you can hit the flea markets. You can still find perfectly good flea markets where you can set up for $10 to $25. Later, you can graduate to a slightly higher-caliber show, whose fees might be from $50 to $100. A lot of people just do shows. It's the exception, actually, having a retail shop. You're tied down and have the overhead."

Adam says that many people get started in the business as they prepare for retirement. They ease into it the last five or ten years of their working careers and then do it as a retirement business to supplement their pension and social security income.

He also feels that it is a recession-resistant business. When times are hard, antiques are a better buy than new items. People shop more carefully, and even noncollectors who just want to get good practical furniture, tools, or gifts will often look for antiques to fill their needs.

Choosing Your Specialty

There are probably thousands of different branches in the antiques and collectibles business. You can take any particular area that interests you—whether it be local history, silver making, the history of advertising, woodworking, tools, lace making, or photographica—and turn that area into a specialty and a whole business. "Look for an area you love," Adam advises. "Learn more about it, and concentrate in it.

"I specialize in about five or six areas I happen to have a particular love and feeling for—antique buttons, costume jewelry from the Victorian era through the forties, 1910 postcards, fountain pens, sterling silver, and antique beads. We also carry some oak furniture, glassware, and photographica. Pastimes is relatively small, but it looks like a well-organized and cleaned-up flea market." In addition, Adam's website, www.pastimes.com, offers online auctions and a "What's It Worth" link, where people can send pictures of items and receive online appraisals of their value.

Avoiding the Pitfalls

Adam is a firm believer that in this business, the less money you have the better. He tells a cautionary tale about a former competitor. "I knew a young man who had inherited $50,000. This was many years ago when that was really a lot of money. He went out and bought every exquisite piece of furniture he could find. I remember at the auctions I was very jealous; he could outbid everybody. He opened up a shop with all those beautiful things, but he couldn't sell them because he'd paid too much for them. Through experience, you have to develop knowledge of what the market will bear. There's no substitute for the actual buying and selling of merchandise to learn about the market and pricing. There are thousands of antique price guides, but this is something you can't really learn by the book. It's best to get into it gradually, go to a lot of antique shows and shops, compare prices, do your homework."

And you have to be careful about where you buy your merchandise, Adam warns. It's vital to make sure the auctioneers and dealers are reputable. "There's a great deal of dishonesty in the business," he admits. "A dealer might misrepresent an item's condition or authenticity. It's easy to get caught." Several collectors were stung by a local dealer who sold alleged turn-of-the-century German lithographs in mint condition. Despite their confidence that these items were authentic, the collectors learned that they were reproductions after buying them in huge quantities for seven to ten dollars each.

Adam himself had an unforeseen situation. As he describes it, "I was selling some red-colored Fiestaware, a very popular deco dinnerware made by Homer Laughlin in the thirties, forties, and fifties. It turned out to be radioactive. Some of the glazes had been made with uranium."

The Upside of the Business

Adam loves what he's doing, always chasing after the next bargain, enjoying the wonderful thrill of the hunt, that feeling you get looking for treasures. "It keeps you excited and fueled up when you're unloading your van in the cold rain or you're stuck in the mud at an auction."

Adam was hooked on collecting antiques after he attended his first auction. Perhaps the style of the auctioneer had something to do with it. For a look at what life is like from the other side of the gavel, you will find a profile of an auctioneer later in this chapter.

Mary Ptak, Vintage Clothing Dealer

Most children love to play dress up, and Mary Ptak, co-owner of the Stock Exchange, a vintage clothing shop in Fort Lauderdale, Florida, was no exception. "I wanted to spend all my time in people's attics," Mary confesses. "I was mainly interested in finding old-style clothing. When I was in college in the sixties, I would just literally knock on strangers' doors and ask them if I could clean out their attics. In those days, they were usually delighted for you to do that."

But times have changed, and people are much more aware of the treasures they might have stored away. "Gone are the days when you could pick up something for twenty-five cents or less," Mary says.

Mary and her partner, Carol Levin, have been in business since 1986. They were both dissatisfied with their jobs, and one day they just decided to take the plunge. Carol loves the sales end of the business, dealing with the customers, and Mary satisfies her shopping urges by traveling around the country as the Stock Exchange's buyer. Their personal business preferences allow for a good division of duties.

Over the years, they've managed to build up an international clientele, including collectors from Japan, Germany, and England.

Mary describes their customers as an eclectic mix. People from England and Japan buy everything they can find from the fifties. The most serious collectors buy clothes from the thirties through the fifties—Joan Crawford, Great Gatsby, and Garbo styles with big padded shoulders and lots of sparkly glitz. Some of their customers are Victorian period collectors.

Mary says that in general, most people want the article they're buying to be useful, something they can actually wear. Local teens are frequent customers. As Mary says, "The kids are always a little more savvy than the general public, and they start fashion trends with their regular street clothes. I used to be able to buy what I liked; now I have to think in terms of my customers' needs."

The Stock Exchange carries clothes ranging in price from $5 for an Indian cotton gauze blouse from the sixties to a $2,000 Schiaparelli gown. It also handles rentals, outfits murder mysteries, and has supplied the costumes for several major television shows and motion pictures, including *Key West*, *Cape Fear*, and *Wrestling Ernest Hemingway*.

How It's Done

Mary travels all over the country to look for just the right pieces. She also has built up a network of people who ship her good finds.

"I learned what was collectible from being in the business a long time," Mary explains. "You have to have a good eye to pick what people want, and you have to change with the times—trends are constantly changing, and you can't always be buying the same things."

For anyone considering a similar business, Mary cautions that it is important to buy clothes that are in excellent condition, unless it's something that's really ancient and people would expect to be damaged. "And you also need a huge amount of stock. When we started out we had very little, but we took consignments then, and because I'm a fanatic shopper, it didn't take long to build it up."

Mary and Carol also managed to build a first-class reputation. "We make an effort to pay people what they deserve for their merchandise. It's one of the reasons we've been so successful."

The Finances Involved

The Stock Exchange is a classic example of laughing all the way to the bank. In 1986, no one would give the two women a business loan. "They didn't think we'd make it," Mary says with just a touch of righteous indignation in her voice.

The two partners have since opened another store in a popular shopping area in Fort Lauderdale. Jezebel, as they've called it, carries upscale vintage clothing, accessories, and antiques.

Mary is kept very busy with the two stores. The one thing she doesn't have time to do anymore is hunt through people's attics. These days she can hire other people to do that.

Art and Antiques Appraisal

Like the collectors we have met in this chapter, many other self-starters dream of finding their niche in the world of antiques and art. Has "Antiques Roadshow" made an armchair appraiser of you? If you can't stay away from tag sales and flea markets and find yourself looking at items with a critical eye, wondering if they might have some hidden value or fascinating history, then a career in art and antiques appraisal might be for you.

The Skills You'll Need

Those who appraise art and antiques are called personal property appraisers; they establish a written opinion of the value of an item for a client. There are certain skills that are beneficial to anyone interested in pursuing this field, which could be nicely combined with entrepreneurial skills to add up to an interesting career.

An appraiser needs good analytical skills and the ability to work with numbers. Interpersonal skills are also very important, since appraisers usually deal directly with clients, and strong writing skills are needed to compose reports.

According to the Appraisal Foundation, a nonprofit educational organization authorized by Congress to set standards and qualifications in the field, most personal property appraisers are required to have a certain number of hours of training and experience in order to practice. To become a designated appraiser, you must also pass a comprehensive examination. Several appraisal organizations award designations following completion of a specific course of training done through the organization.

The Appraisal Foundation's Appraiser Qualifications Board has set voluntary minimum criteria for personal property appraisers. At present, the recommendation is for at least 1,800 hours of experience, 120 hours of education, and successful completion of a written examination. Most appraisers get their required experience hours by working as apprentices with established appraisers.

Since most appraisers receive their training through professional organizations, a college degree is not required for this career. A degree might be a requirement for advanced designations by certain organizations but is not a prerequisite for entering the field.

Where You Might Work

The services of personal property appraisers are used by a variety of clients. Museums, insurance companies, and government agencies all need to determine the value of items for which they are responsible.

As more and more people wonder about the value of those old collectibles in the attic, as sales of art and antiques continue to increase, so does the need for personal property appraisers. There are many private companies that offer appraisal services, but this growing field could provide many opportunities for self-starters. Many appraisers work independently as consultants or freelancers, dividing their time among various clients.

Jim Ridolfi, Auctioneer

"I have this nice oak roll-top desk, how about a five-hundred-dollar bid, get five hundred, get five hundred, get two and a half, start us off, give us a hundred, give a hundred," is part of the chant you'll hear from auctioneer Jim Ridolfi, owner of the Aspon Trading Company in Troy, Pennsylvania.

As Jim describes it, every professional auctioneer has his own chant, a way of announcing the items and handling the bids. For his chant, Jim says, "I try not to use too many words—the people won't understand you. What they're listening for is the numbers. You learn a basic method at auctioneer training school, and then you take it and refine it and make it into your own."

Training for Auctioneers

Training programs for auctioneers can last from two weeks to several months, depending on state requirements. Some states do not have licensing requirements; others have very strict regulations. Most training programs cover the many types of auctions, such as estate sales, automotive, antiques, real estate, livestock, and machinery. In addition, students study public speaking, advertising, crowd control, sales, and business skills.

There are several national auctioneering schools. The most well known is the Missouri Auction School, an internationally recognized establishment that has trained auctioneers for nearly one hundred years. Before choosing a program, however, it is advisable to check on which schools your state will accept. Some states only license auctioneers who have graduated from schools in that state. Contact your state licensing board or the National Auctioneers Association (listed in Appendix A) for information.

How Jim Got Started

Like Jim Ridolfi, many auctioneers are also antiques dealers. Jim specializes in old phonographs and radios and especially loves mid- to late-nineteenth-century items. Jim became an auctioneer in 1992. He advertises his services in newspapers and has worked with other antiques dealers, estate attorneys, and will executors.

The Finances Involved

Auctioneers may hold their events indoors in hotel ballrooms, outside in farmers' fields, or in the backyards of estates. Some locations are provided rent-free, whereas for others there may be a charge.

Auctioneers work on a percentage basis, earning between 15 and 30 percent of the price of each item sold.

Related Work in the Field

In addition to your future role as an auctioneer, you might find yourself supervising other employees, such as these:

- **Runners** move the items for sale from the holding area to the stage.
- **Floor managers** supervise the runners, let them know which items are going up next, and take care of any other details so the auctioneer is not distracted.
- **Clerks** make a record of the proceedings and handle the numbering of lots and bidders.
- **Cashiers** collect the money.
- **Security guards** watch over the sold items while they're waiting to be picked up.
- **Caterers** provide refreshments for the audience and staff.
- **Advertisers and marketers** help the auctioneer to publicize his or her services and particular auction events.
- **Catalogers** work with large estates, organizing the items and taking precise inventories.
- **Appraisers** help authenticate and place a value on particular items.

- **Furniture refinishers and restorers**, although not usually directly involved with an auction, find work with dealers or private individuals giving life back to old or damaged items.
- **Flea market and antiques show organizers** coordinate the big events that attract thousands of people. They handle every detail, including advertising, allocating space, and collecting fees.

CHAPTER FOUR

Service Industry Careers

Perhaps the greatest variety of opportunities for self-starters exists in the service industry. This sector of the economy employs the highest number of people in the United States, with lots of room for entrepreneurs.

Because it is such a wide-open occupational category, it would be impossible to name all the options. A few key businesses are covered in this chapter, and other types of service endeavors appear in various chapters throughout the book.

How to Choose Your Service

Perhaps you know you want to enter into some sort of service enterprise, but you're not sure of the working conditions the different fields offer or which area would best suit your personality, skills, and lifestyle. There are several factors to consider when deciding which sector of the service industry to pursue. Each field carries with it different levels of responsibility and commitment. To identify occupations that will match your expectations, you need to know what the different services entail.

To help narrow the field, ask yourself the following questions:

- How much of a "people person" are you? Do you prefer to work face-to-face with clients or customers, or are you more comfortable with telephone contact?
- Do you want a desk job, or would you prefer to be out and about?

- How much time are you willing to commit to training? Some skills can be learned on the job or in a year or two of formal training; others can take considerably longer.
- How much money do you expect to earn after you graduate and after you have a few years' experience under your belt? Salaries and earnings vary greatly in each service profession. Knowing what your expectations are, then comparing them to the realities of the work, will help you make informed choices.

Hairstylists and Cosmetologists

Every year consumers spend millions of dollars on beauty and physical fitness. Cosmetics, exercise equipment, and health clubs are factors in nearly everyone's budget. Acquiring the right look costs money, as we seek the perfect hairstyles and nails or just the right makeup as well as the most fine-tuned bodies we can drum into shape. Owning your own beauty salon or having your own freelance business is a route many self-starters follow.

As people increasingly demand styles that are better suited to their individual characteristics, they rely more and more on hairstylists and cosmetologists. Although tastes and fashions change from year to year, the basic job duties remain the same—to help people look their best.

Hairstylists and cosmetologists primarily shampoo, cut, and style hair. They may also advise patrons on how to care for their own hair. As more and more techniques become available, they straighten hair, change its color, and add highlights, all in the attempt to create that perfect look sought by a client. Most hairstylists who own their salons still work with clients in addition to their responsibilities for the day-to-day operation of the shop.

The last decade has seen an increase in the number of specialized services available to consumers. Manicurists and pedicurists, often called nail technicians, work exclusively on nails and provide manicures, pedicures, coloring, and nail extensions. Many beauty salons employ nail technicians, although shops that cater exclusively to nail care are common.

Training

Although all fifty states require stylists and cosmetologists to be licensed, the qualifications necessary to obtain a license vary. Generally, a person must have graduated from a state-licensed barber or cosmetology school and be at least sixteen years old. Some states require applicants to pass a physical examination.

Education requirements also vary from state to state. Some states require graduation from high school, whereas others require only an eighth-grade education. In a few states, completion of an apprenticeship can substitute for formal education, but very few stylists or cosmetologists learn their skills in this way. Applicants for a license usually are required to pass a written test and demonstrate an ability to perform basic barbering or cosmetology services.

Some states have reciprocity agreements that allow licensed stylists and cosmetologists to move their practices between states without additional formal training. Other states do not recognize training or licenses obtained elsewhere. Consequently, it is a good idea to review the laws of the state in which you want to work before entering a training program.

Many public and private vocational schools offer day or evening classes in barbering and cosmetology. Full-time programs usually last nine to twenty-four months, and an apprenticeship program can last from one to three years.

Formal training programs include classroom study, demonstrations, and practical work. Students study the basic techniques of haircutting, shaving, facial massage, and hair and scalp treatments. Under supervision, students also practice on customers in school clinics. Students attend lectures on the use and care of instruments, sanitation and hygiene, and recognition of certain skin ailments.

Instruction is also given in communication, sales, and general business practices. There are advanced courses for experienced barbers in hairstyling, coloring, and the sale and service of hairpieces. Most schools teach unisex styling.

After graduating from a training program, students can take the state licensing examination, which consists of a written test and, in some cases, a practical test of cosmetology skills. A few states include an oral examination in which the applicant is asked to explain the procedures he or she is following while taking the practical test. In some states, a separate examination is given for applicants who want only a manicurist or facial-care license.

Many schools help their graduates find employment. During their first months on the job, new workers perform relatively simple tasks, such as giving shampoos, or are assigned to perform the simpler hairstyling patterns. Once they have demonstrated their skills, they are gradually permitted to perform the more complicated tasks such as giving shaves, coloring hair, or applying permanents.

Michael Silvestri, Hairstylist

Michael Silvestri has been in the business for more than thirty-five years, both as a salaried hairstylist and as the owner of his own salons.

"It's great. It's really interesting work," says Michael. "I love people. If you didn't, you couldn't stay in this business. Today, most of my best friends are people I've met in the industry, mostly clients."

Michael gets great satisfaction from working with clients, particularly new ones to whom he can give lots of attention. As he says, "It's great to take someone and make her over, make her look totally different than when she came in. That's the fun part."

The Finances Involved. "The advantage, of course, to being an owner is that you have the opportunity to make a lot more money," Michael states. "If it all clicks, you've got it good. When I had the two salons going and we had twenty-six employees, we were doing very well. And, of course, there's the satisfaction when you do well—starting a business and watching it grow."

On the other hand, Michael cautions that business—and, therefore, the money—often fluctuates. "Because the employees come and go, you could go from twenty-six employees down to fifteen, but you have the same overhead. The hours are terrible, and you need a huge financial outlay to start a business. You'd probably need at least $100,000 now to do it."

The money a salaried stylist makes depends on several factors. According to Michael, "When you're not an owner, you can pick and choose where you're going to work and set your own hours. If you don't want to work six hours, you can work four. It's up to you."

Of course, a hairstylist's skill level and talent play a big part in determining how much money he or she can earn. This includes not only styling skills, but also the ability to communicate with clients and keep them coming back. The salon where the stylist works is another factor. The type of salon and its location can make a difference in how much money a hairstylist makes. Small neighborhood salons generally pay less than upscale salons in large cities or in high-end department stores.

As Michael Silvestri describes the financial situation, "You'd make any combination of a salary, plus commission, plus tips. Commissions can run from 40 to 70 percent. Base salary could be as low as a couple of hundred a week—just something to get you started. Tips would fluctuate wildly." In many salons, a shampoo assistant might earn only $100 per week, and a stylist might earn five times that amount.

The Realities of the Job. Michael emphasizes that establishing a good relationship with a client is a big part of the job. "In dealing with clients, you have to spend time with them, learn about them, and help them get over any past bad experiences they've had at the hairdresser's. You might decide what you believe will look good on them, but then you have to be able to convince them that it will work. Sometimes it takes more than one appointment to get comfortable with each other. But make one mistake, and you could lose that client forever."

There are also physical stresses that go along with the work. Hairdressers spend most of their time standing, so general good health and stamina are important for personal comfort. Some styling products contain chemicals that might cause irritation after prolonged exposure; most stylists wear protective gloves and aprons when necessary to prevent adverse reactions.

Most full-time hairstylists work a forty-hour week, but longer hours are not uncommon, especially for self-employed workers. Work schedules often include evenings and weekends, when most salons are busiest. In addition, many work on holidays or Sundays to prepare clients for weddings or other special events.

Michael says honestly that owning a beauty salon does have its difficulties. He found that managing his employees was not always easy, since it involved dealing with many different personalities and attitudes. And it is hard to let stylists go, since usually their clients will follow them to their new locations, taking business away from your establishment.

How Michael Got Started. Michael Silvestri was working on Wall Street as a stock transfer clerk, a job that he did not enjoy. His uncle, a barber, convinced Michael to attend school to study hairstyling. He enrolled in a private school at age seventeen, completing a one-year program.

Male hairdressers were not very common at the time, so Michael worked as an apprentice in order to get a start in the business. He worked as a shampoo assistant, and although he did not make much money, he feels that he did learn a lot about the business.

Michael took another one-month course and was then hired as a hairdresser at the shop where he had worked as an apprentice. Three years later, he opened his first salon. He kept that shop for six years until he moved out of New York. He managed a salon in Philadelphia for ten years and ultimately opened two more shops of his own. Several years later Michael sold both shops and began to work as an employee in another salon.

Some Advice from Michael. Michael understands the nature of the relationship between hairdresser and client, and he gave his new employees a pep talk when they were hired. He reminded them that a new client is most likely "scared to death" and that it is part of the stylist's job to make the client feel comfortable and to establish trust and confidence. Michael says that with new clients, "You have to spend time consulting with them, taking their lifestyle into consideration, the shape of their face, and what kind of hair they have. Then you can go to work, but not before."

In addition, Michael emphasizes the need for independence and ambition. As he says, "You can't be afraid. You're going to function as an independent contractor for your whole career, so you have to be able to take care of yourself.

"Then you have to decide that you're willing to work hard enough to make this work. If you're lazy, you won't make any money. It will take a while to build up your clientele, as well as your skills and confidence. You have to be prepared for one or two lean years."

Robin Landry, Esthetician

Whereas a cosmetologist is trained primarily in hair care, an esthetician works exclusively with skin care. Estheticians give facials, full-body treatments, and head and neck massages, as well as remove hair through waxing.

Robin Landry is a skin-care professional working freelance as an independent contractor.

"It doesn't look as if I work for myself because I operate out of two different salons," she explains, "but in actuality, I do. I'm paid on commission. The salons give me a workplace—I don't have to pay rent or other overhead expenses—they provide me with all my products and supplies, and for that they take a 35 percent cut. I also get tips and a percentage—an average of 15 percent—on the beauty products I sell to my clients.

"In addition, being on the premises provides me with a captive audience, so to speak. But of course, once they put the clients into my hands, it's up to me to make sure they keep coming back."

Robin enjoys her work, particularly making a client feel good. She also gets to see immediate results of her work, which is especially gratifying. Robin acknowledges that working on someone's skin is a very personal matter, and she understands that it is often difficult for people to ask for help in that area. Once they do, however, and they see the results of Robin's labor, they come to trust her.

Establishing a good relationship with clients is a big part of Robin's success: "To keep your clients happy requires professionalism. A lot of people can give a good facial, but a good bedside manner and my professionalism really make a big difference. And I keep them coming back with a good product. I believe in what I sell and what I do. That says a lot to my clients."

Behind the Scenes. "Giving the actual facial is a very relaxing hour and fifteen minutes, for both my clients and myself," Robin acknowledges. "Clients do remark on that. They're very envious of my silent, quiet job. But they only see that side of it. They don't see the frustrations."

Even though administering treatments can be relaxing, Robin's overall schedule is very busy. She works a four-day week, including one twelve-hour day, one nine-hour day, and two eight-hour days. She allows herself three days off each week to avoid burnout. Clients are often demanding, asking many questions about the products and services, voicing concerns about treatments, and wanting to share their own experiences with Robin.

In addition to keeping up with a hectic schedule, Robin has to sell products and maintain files on each client. The files are her way of knowing which treatments she has given and which products her clients have purchased. Selling the products is an important element of her job, since a good part of Robin's money is made through retail.

One of Robin's biggest frustrations is clients who don't keep their appointments. Robin has tried to deal with this situation, but it is not easy. She established a policy that clients who fail to give twenty-four hours' notice of a cancellation are billed 50 percent of the treatment cost, but she finds it difficult to enforce.

As an esthetician, Robin understands that her own appearance is a very important factor in her success. Few clients are willing to trust their skin care to someone whose own appearance is sloppy or unprofessional. As Robin states, "Your performance and your appearance always have to be a '10.' That can be tricky, keeping yourself together when you're running like a crazy person all day. Your hair falls out of its scrunchy, and your lipstick wears off, and it's four hours before you have time to put more on. Always make sure to do that, though. I wear a cake powder so my skin always looks good, and I make sure I always have lipstick on.

"But it feels good, being your own boss, and being in charge of your own success."

The Finances Involved. Robin charges different prices for various services. For example, a facial costs approximately $50, while waxing ranges from $15 to $100, and makeup application can cost up to $55. In addition, clients often spend $150 or so on products. As Robin says, it is important to keep products in stock, or she can lose the sale. She has learned that it is best if she does the ordering herself, to avoid any problems with salon owners not stocking the products she needs.

How Robin Got Started. Robin Landry was studying massage therapy when she fell and broke her wrist. The injury left her unable to work and in occupational therapy for two years. When she was able to return to work, Robin had jobs with a chiropractor and a dentist, and she found that she really enjoyed the one-on-one patient care.

What Robin did not enjoy, however, was feeling unappreciated by her employers. It was this feeling that made her decide to do "something for myself, with myself, by myself, and be able to thank myself for it."

Robin returned to school to study skin care. Her choice of programs was influenced by her interest in massage therapy over any other area of the esthetic industry. She studied for six months at a private career institute, concentrating on skin care, makeup, and waxing. Upon completion of the program, she passed her state's licensing exam. Since that time, Robin has supplemented her knowledge with continuing education courses and seminars offered by product manufacturers.

Some Tips from Robin. Based on her own experience, Robin says, "I would highly recommend a career in skin care. I consider it more glamorous and less taxing than working with hair and nails."

From a financial perspective, she feels that it is more lucrative to work on a percentage basis out of an established salon than to rent your own space. She did rent her own shop during her first year in business and lost money.

"You can make a good living, but it's unpredictable," Robin says. "You never know how much you're going to earn. You need to give yourself time to gradually and consistently build up your business.

"Above all else, you have to keep yourself knowledgeable about your work and your products. People will believe in you if you show them that you're confident in what you're doing."

Personal Trainers

Attaining the perfect body (or at least a better one) is part of many people's overall health and beauty goals. Toward this end, more and more consumers employ the services of personal trainers. Personal trainers work in health clubs, spas, and gyms or in private practice, working on a one-to-one basis with clients.

The Training You'll Need

To meet safety standards and insurance, state, and local regulations, most health club–type settings require their instructors and trainers to have appropriate qualifications or licenses. Personal trainers hold a great deal of responsibility for their clients' welfare and must be fully trained in what they do.

There are a few routes trainers can take to learn the craft and become certified. Many colleges and universities offer exercise science or exercise physiology programs. The American Council on Exercise (ACE) and the American College of Sports Medicine (ACSM) both administer certification exams.

Both organizations' tests have written and practical components. The practical test consists of submax testing, where you are evaluated while you monitor a client's heart rate and blood pressure. You also put your client through a workout, and your spotting techniques and interaction with the client are judged.

A training program can take two to eight weeks or up to four years, if you pursue a bachelor's degree. Once you are a personal trainer you need continuing education credits to keep up your certification. One option is the Online Learning Center, offered by the ACE. This is an interactive Web-based training program that allows you to earn ACE-approved continuing education credits.

Frank Cassisa, Certified Personal Trainer

Frank Cassisa is a certified personal trainer at a national health and fitness chain. He works as an independent contractor.

"Fitness instruction is just like computers: it's always changing; there's always something new coming out. To be the best trainer, you have to stay on top of everything."

Frank finds health clubs to be the best working environment. The club's customers form a ready-made client base. A trainer who works out of a health club can also maintain a private practice, either at his or her own place or working in clients' homes.

What the Job Involves. Frank says that a certified personal trainer must be aware of many things before beginning to work with a client. Complete knowledge of the human body, its abilities and limitations, and each client's individual needs must be considered. One program does not work for every client. Frank says that clients with special considerations—such as diabetes, arthritis, or pregnancy—need different training programs from others.

A certified personal trainer knows about nutrition and kinesiology, the study of the movement of the body, and how the muscles respond to various exercises. Trainers learn first aid and must be certified in CPR. The trainer must also check all equipment to ensure safety before a client uses it.

Simply wanting to work with a trainer does not necessarily mean that it's possible to do so. Sometimes a trainer must refuse a client based on health-related issues. Frank describes the initial contact with a client: "With the general population, people who want to improve their fitness, we first have to take a health history, get a doctor's name and number, and ask the right questions — age, smoking, any history of health risk factors. If we feel a person is not ready for a training program, we'll say so and suggest consulting a doctor for a physical."

If a client is physically ready for training, Frank conducts an assessment of overall physical fitness, including flexibility, muscular strength and endurance, cardiovascular endurance, and body composition. Training sessions usually last one hour, with clients working with Frank once or twice a week.

How Frank Got Started. Physical fitness has always been Frank's hobby, and now he is able to earn his living from it. He studied through the ACE and passed its two-part exam, the written and practical tests.

Although fitness is now Frank's profession, it is also still his hobby. As he says, "I love to work out and I love to teach people. I work five days a week. When I take my two-hour lunch break, I'm working out. You have to be driven and absorb the whole lifestyle."

The Finances Involved. Personal trainers in health clubs can work on commission or for an hourly rate, earning anywhere from $75 to $200 an hour, depending on the clientele. Trainers can set their own hours, taking as many clients in a day as they choose.

Another consideration for self-employed trainers is insurance. Frank works for a club and is therefore covered under the club's insurance policy. Trainers who work out of their own spaces or in clients' homes, however, must carry their own insurance.

Expert Advice from Frank. Frank understands how important a personal trainer can become to a client. "You need a great attitude, and you have to practice what you preach. To clients you're a friend, father figure, role model. They'll follow someone who has the results they're looking for."

Frank also advises that a personal trainer needs to be caring but firm and must be able to communicate with clients to help them achieve the desired results. As he says, "You need a firm hand but diplomatic skills. You're an instructor, not a dictator."

Other Service Careers

As mentioned earlier, there is a wide spectrum of service careers available for self-starters and entrepreneurs. Further exploration or brainstorming on your part will most likely reveal even more possibilities.

What follows are just two examples of interesting and different self-starter service opportunities.

Genealogists

The study of genealogy, tracing family histories, has grown dramatically in popularity in recent years. Almost everyone has a keen interest in his or her family background. Genealogists interview older family members; visit courthouses, cemeteries, and libraries; and spend hours poring through diaries, old newspaper accounts, marriage licenses, and birth and death certificates.

Many genealogy hobbyists take their interest one step further and become self-employed genealogists, helping others to uncover their family trees. Genealogists are also employed in historical societies and libraries with special genealogy rooms. The Church of Jesus Christ of Latter-Day Saints in Salt Lake City, for example, maintains a huge repository of family information in its Family History Library. The church employs genealogists all over the world and includes genealogists who have been accredited through its own program on a list of freelance researchers. Contact information for the Family History Library is listed in Appendix A.

Other genealogists find work teaching their skills in adult education classes, editing genealogy magazines, or writing books or newspaper columns.

Most genealogists are not formally trained, though specializing in genealogy is possible through some university history and library science programs. Although there is not a specified curriculum for genealogists, the Board for Certification of Genealogists stresses the importance of certification for those interested in seriously pursuing this field. Information on certification requirements and procedures can be obtained from the Board for Certification, listed in Appendix A.

Independent-study courses are offered by various teaching institutions throughout the country. Many local and state genealogy societies sponsor one- and two-day seminars. Information about these seminars is published in the newsletters of both the Federation of Genealogical Societies and the National Genealogical Society. These organizations also hold annual conferences at various sites nationwide. See Appendix A for contact information.

Salaries for Genealogists. According to the Society of Professional Genealogists, most genealogists charge by the hour and bill for out-of-pocket expenses, such as photocopies, telephone calls, travel, and vital-records fees. Hourly rates range from about $15 to $100, with the average between $25 and $60. Fees vary among professionals, depending upon experience, credentials, specialty, and geographic area. Highly skilled experts who specialize in unusually difficult research problems may charge higher rates.

How to Get Started. One of the nice things about genealogy is that you can pursue it on your own before making a commitment to serious study. In this way you can decide whether this is a service that you would enjoy providing.

The National Genealogical Society suggests beginning with your own family tree as an introduction to genealogy and offers the following suggestions for how to get started:

- **Make a chart.** Start with yourself, your parents, your grandparents, and your great-grandparents. This will be the beginning of your family tree.
- **Search for records.** Look for birth, marriage, and death certificates and any other documents that might provide names, dates, and locations. Check your family's Bible records, old letters, and photographs for clues to people's identities and relationships. Label everything you find to make it easier to organize your research.
- **Talk to family members.** Encourage older relatives to talk about their childhoods and relatives, and listen carefully for

clues they might inadvertently drop. Learn good interviewing techniques so you ask questions that elicit the most productive answers. Use a tape recorder or camcorder, and try to verify each fact through a separate source.

- **Visit your local library.** Become familiar with historical and genealogical publications, and contact local historical societies. Check out the state library and the archives in your state capital. Seek out any specialty ethnic or religious libraries, and visit cemeteries.

- **Visit courthouses.** Cultivate friendships with busy court clerks. Ask to see source records, such as wills, deeds, marriage books, and birth and death certificates that are not readily available from family members.

- **Enter into correspondence.** Write to other individuals and societies involved with the same families or regions. Contact foreign embassies in Washington, D.C. Restrict yourself to asking only one question in each letter you send. Include the information you have already uncovered. Include a self-addressed stamped envelope and your e-mail address to encourage replies.

- **Keep painstaking records.** Use printed family group sheets or pedigree charts. Develop a well-organized filing system so you'll be able to easily find your information. Enter your research information into a database if possible. Keep separate records for each family you research.

- **Contact the National Genealogical Society.** Browse its online bookstore for helpful publications. You can enroll in the society's home-study course titled "American Genealogy: A Basic Course" or take a course in the Online Learning Center. Contact information is listed in Appendix A.

Arborists

The preservation and care of trees and shrubs, including woody vines as well as ground cover plantings, is called arboriculture.

Arborists, or tree trimmers, are the experts who take care of trees. They have many responsibilities, including planting and transplanting trees, pruning and trimming them, spraying for insects, treating for diseases, fertilizing, bracing, installing lightning protection, and, when necessary, removing them.

Professional arborists sometimes work independently as consultants. They provide inspections of trees and landscape plants and make reports to insurance companies on tree and other landscape loss due to storm damage, automobile accidents, or vandalism. They can also serve as expert witnesses, providing testimony in court cases.

Consulting arborists are qualified to establish dollar values for trees for the purpose of real estate appraisals. During construction of new property, arborists assist in the preservation of existing trees, prepare specifications for the planting of new trees, and diagnose any problems.

The Work Involved. For the most part, hands-on tree workers perform jobs that require a great deal of physical labor, such as hauling branches and other cumbersome material. They handle heavy and dangerous equipment, such as chain saws, hydraulic pruners, and stump grinders.

Arborists often work from great heights, climbing trees or working from an aerial lift or a cherry picker, a truck-mounted crane with a large bucket on the end in which the worker stands while trimming trees.

Arborists also handle pesticides and chemicals for preventive and corrective measures in the treatment of insect problems or diseases. To apply these pesticides, they must be licensed and follow state and federal laws regulating the use of chemicals.

Way Hoyt, Arborist. Way Hoyt is owner of Tree Trimmers and Associates in Fort Lauderdale, Florida. "The trees are our associates," Way says. "They have a big part in our business."

Way's wife, Geri Hoyt, is the owner of Arborist Supply House, which sells ropes, saddles, pruners, shears, and other equipment for tree workers.

Way has been planting trees since he was about seven years old. "I'm the little kid who ran along the turnpike taking Australian pine saplings out, then transplanting them in my yard. I didn't get in trouble with my folks for doing that until the trees grew to be humongous."

Way has an associate's degree and attended the University of Florida at the research and experimental station in Fort Lauderdale. He has been in business eighteen years.

"I chose self-employment first for financial reasons. But when I was working for other companies, I found out that they were basically doing terrible things to the trees. I went into my own business so I could do proper tree trimming.

"Pruning, done correctly, is the healthiest thing a tree can have done to it. Done incorrectly, as in stubs, nubs, rips, tears, flesh cuts, too much green being removed, or not enough attention paid to structural material, it can be the worst treatment for the tree."

One of Way's concerns about the profession is the abundance of what he calls "hat-rack specialists." "This is a term used for mutilating trees, and that's what an awful lot of tree services continue to do," Way explains. "There are right ways and wrong ways of treating trees, and there is a world of information on tree trimming, but it's been my experience that a large percentage of tree trimmers don't know anything about it. Anybody who can work a chain saw thinks he can trim a tree, and anybody can hang out a shingle and call himself an arborist, even if he's not. All that is required is a small fee to the county for an occupational license, and then you can legally call yourself a tree expert."

Way is also concerned about conservation. His company's motto is "A tree company working with our environment and associated ecology, performing tree work both scientifically and aesthetically."

Way encourages people to attend good programs and get the proper training. He also teaches courses at Flamingo Gardens on arboriculture, tree identification, and what happens inside a tree when it's been damaged on the outside.

In addition, he has been asked on numerous occasions to appear as an expert witness in court. He talks about his most recent case. "A fellow was driving east during stormy weather along a four-lane highway with a median strip. The trunk of a black olive tree split and fell on his car as he was driving by at about forty-five to fifty miles per hour. He was seriously injured, permanently paralyzed in fact.

"A few months before the accident, the tree had been trimmed. I took a look at the tree and saw indications of serious structural problems. The trimming done was not adequate. The trimmer should have notified the property owner of a possible dangerous situation but didn't. The professional maintenance company and the condominium complex that own the tree are being sued.

"When I go into court, I'll talk about the tree and the structure and how it was an accident waiting to happen."

Summing up his feelings about his profession, Way says, "You can certainly make a career out of it and never stop learning. And it's very satisfying. You can step back and look at what you have accomplished and know that you did a nice job, helping a tree."

The Training You'll Need. Requirements vary, but helpers, ground workers, and climbers seldom need a formal education. However, a high school diploma is desirable. To advance in the field, an arborist must demonstrate knowledge of arboriculture, biology, botany, entomology, and plant pathology. Vocational schools and two-year community colleges offer training in this increasingly complex work. On-the-job training is equally important for a successful career.

All state environmental departments require licensing before you can use pesticides. You will also need a valid driver's license, preferably a commercial license for driving trucks and tractors.

The International Society of Arboriculture grants prestigious certification to arborists with experience and education who pass a comprehensive written examination. See Appendix A for contact information.

Salaries for Arborists. Just as the duties of arborists vary, so do salaries. Physical laborers, who generally work the hardest, are paid from $12,000 to $20,000 per year for ground work and from $15,000 to $30,000 for climbing. Supervisors or consulting arborists, who rely more on their years of experience and expertise than physical strength, can be paid $35,000 and up. Self-employed consultants usually charge by the hour or determine a set rate for a project.

CHAPTER FIVE

Careers in the Limelight

s there a bit of the performer in you? Are you looking to do something unusual, something different, something that will definitely not tie you to a forty-hour week?

Many innovative people have combined their desire for self-employment with other talents or acquired skills. With a good imagination, a dedicated self-starter can bring in extra income or carve out a specialized career. Here are a few successful and unusual ventures that might spark some ideas of your own.

Walking Tours

If you're comfortable talking with small groups of people, like to walk, know how to conduct research, and can put together a one-to two-hour presentation, then starting a walking tour might be a fun way to bring in some additional earnings.

There are different kinds of tours you can organize, depending on how rich your area is in history and local color. Here are just a few themes to consider:

- **Mystery walking tour**—highlighting locations of unusual or unsolved crimes or the homes of notorious residents.
- **Architectural walking tour**—featuring homes and buildings of unusual interest. Some examples of well-suited areas are the Art Deco District in Miami, the French

Quarter in New Orleans, or the stately neighborhoods of
Charleston, South Carolina.

- **Literary walking tour**—focusing on the homes and lives of
  famous local writers.

Mystery Walking Tours

Basically, the leader of a mystery walking tour escorts a group of
paying people to designated sites and landmarks in a particular
area. At each stop the leader gives a talk on that specific spot,
telling about its history or notoriety and answering questions.

Mystery walking tours are usually organized around a particular theme. Stops on the route may include homes of famous mystery writers or focus on where crimes or scandals occurred. For
example, a tour of Boston could follow the killing spree route of
the Boston Strangler. The popularity of *Midnight in the Garden of
Good and Evil* has spawned several tours in Savannah, Georgia.
New Orleans is ripe with legend, mystery, and intrigue, and even
an island as small as Key West has had its share of titillating incidents. Some tours focus on the paranormal, others on actual doc-
umented events.

How far you can go with this idea depends in part on where you
live and how active criminals or mystery writers are in your area.

Follow these ten steps to get started:

1. **Research your area.** Visit the public library, check out
   courthouse records, or ask to be allowed into the newspaper morgue. Search the Internet for past events or notorious residents, but remember they must all be within
   walking distance of each other.
2. **Decide on the tour length.** From your research, determine
   how much information you have to support a tour. Then
   organize your information to follow the different stops
   you'll make. Allow ten minutes or so for each spot. Get as
   many juicy details as possible. Gory and gruesome details

will work well, too. Remember, everyone loves a good mystery!

3. **Decide on a price.** A ninety-minute to two-hour walking tour costs on average $20 per person. You can give discounts for children or senior citizens. The more people you have in your group, the more you'll make.

4. **Decide how often you will offer tours.** Every Saturday morning? Sunday afternoons? Some of the scarier tours are offered at night, when darkness adds to the sense of mystery. If the area warrants it, you could run one or two a day. It's up to you.

5. **Make a dry run.** Walk the tour with friends and family and practice your presentation. It's unlikely that you'll be able to enter any of the buildings without making some sort of arrangement with the owners, so be sure to pick out a spot where you and your group can pause to talk. Under a shady tree is good for summer days, but be careful not to block vehicular or pedestrian traffic.

6. **Check with local officials.** Find out if there are any zoning restrictions or occupational licenses or permits you'll need.

7. **Prepare your pamphlets.** You'll need to design and print a brochure that details your tour, how people can contact you, the times and dates you operate, and how much the tour will cost. Be sure to mention whether any part of your tour includes steep or uneven terrain that participants should know about in advance; you don't want anyone falling behind or unable to complete the tour. And, though it might seem obvious, mention that customers should wear comfortable walking shoes.

8. **Set up marketing outlets.** You'll want to stop in at various hotels, visitor centers, chambers of commerce, historical societies, and any other spots frequented by tourists or residents to ask if you can leave promotional pamphlets on display for prospective customers. Your plan will most

likely be met with enthusiasm. Establishments that cater to tourists are usually glad to help advertise events. Many hotels already keep racks in their lobbies filled with pamphlets for various local attractions.

9. **Find additional ways to promote your tour.** Create a press release to send to newspapers; most local papers regularly publish a calendar of events. Contact local radio stations and cable television stations and drop in at bookstores (a favorite hangout for mystery buffs). Make arrangements for your tour to be included on Internet sites about your city's attractions.

10. **Equip yourself for walking.** Invest in a pair of good walking shoes, dig out the sunscreen, and get ready to have fun.

David Kaufelt's Key West Walking Tour

David Kaufelt is a noted mystery writer and the founder of the annual Key West Literary Seminar. While organizing the first year's events, David put together a mystery walking tour of the island to entertain seminar participants.

Here is David's description of starting his tour: "Key West is the scene of many funny mysteries and murders that have never been solved. I'd been reading about them . . . and I'd done some research for an article I wrote on the subject, and from that came the idea to start the Mystery Walking Tour. We needed some money for the Key West Literary Seminar, and I thought that this would be a good way to raise some funds. We've always done a tour of great writers' houses in Key West, and the mystery tour is an offshoot of that."

David did some research on some of the stranger events of Key West's past. For example, a young man and an older man shared a mansion around the corner from David's former home. The two fought quite often, and no one had seen the younger man for quite some time. It came to light that the younger man was an alcoholic and had died, but the older man didn't acknowledge his death.

As David describes it, "He thought the younger man was just being ornery. So he'd go get him food every day and told people how he would never speak to him. But then we all started smelling something strange, and the police were finally notified. The young guy had been dead for months and had almost melted into the linoleum floor in the kitchen. The older man's mind had gone, and his family came and took him away and put him someplace."

David's tours also include the cemetery, where there is always an interesting murder to talk about.

Some Advice for Tour Guides. David Kaufelt offers some advice for anyone interested in starting a mystery walking tour. He recommends that you do your research very well and be entertaining. You need to be able to tell an anecdote with a punch line to keep your audience interested.

It is helpful to get an organization behind you, such as Mystery Writers of America or Sisters in Crime. You can search the Internet for organizations in keeping with the theme of your tour. You might also become associated with an Elderhostel program in your area. People come to a city to learn, and such organizations can put together different events for them.

Make sure you have something with which to identify yourself for people who will be meeting you on a street corner. It could be a T-shirt with a logo printed on it or a banner you can wave.

Murder Mystery Dinners

The last several years have seen the rise of a form of entertainment especially designed to appeal to mystery buffs. No longer do restaurant goers have only their companions and food to keep them occupied. Some enterprising entrepreneurs have arranged for a waiter or waitress, a cook, or perhaps even someone dining at your table to keel over dead in front of your eyes—shot, stabbed, or maybe even poisoned.

Whodunit? That's for diners to figure out. Here is a look at two professional companies that produce mystery theater dinner shows.

Grace Bentley Theatrical Productions

Adriana and Rick Rogers own Grace Bentley Theatrical Productions, based in Carmel, New York. They formed the company in 1999 to produce mystery theater shows.

According to Adriana, their original intention was to rent scripts from an established distributor, but she and Rick found the scripts to be below their standards. They had a particular level of entertainment in mind, and the scripts they were renting just didn't meet their expectations. Adriana says that too many were "lowbrow, not family-oriented. I would have been embarrassed to put my name on the shows."

Adriana and Rick wanted to present family-oriented shows that they could feel comfortable performing for school groups as well as for adults. After realizing that there weren't any available scripts that they wanted to use, they decided to write their own material. They had written a play before and knew they could write material that they would be proud to perform before any audience. As Adriana says, "Plays are like your children, and you don't trust your children to just anyone."

They started with a show set in the 1940s, *The Zoot Suit Swing Time Murders*. The show centers on a band performing in a dance hall; one of the members is murdered. There are lots of clues to help the audience figure out the killer's identity, and plenty of incentive as well. Audience members get to participate in the action, as the cast interacts with diners, dropping hints and clues, trying to throw the dining detectives off the track. Once the murder is solved, prizes are given to those who correctly deduce the identity of the killer.

Based on the success of this show, Rick and Adriana wrote two more scripts. *Murder at the Sock Hop* is set in the 1950s, and *Death at the Disco* is set in the 1970s. They employ about fifteen actors, including understudies. Most of their actors work in more than one show.

Adriana acts in all three shows, and Rick serves as an understudy. His main job during performances is to run the soundboard, so he prefers not to act since it means he would have to do two jobs at once. Rick would rather devote his time to the sound system to be sure that it is run correctly for each show. Adriana and Rick do all the backstage work themselves.

When Grace Bentley first began, Adriana placed ads in newspapers to attract customers. Now, however, all of the company's advertising is either by word of mouth or through the establishments where they perform. For instance, audience members often approach Adriana and Rick after a show to ask if they will perform at a fund-raiser or similar event. The organization sponsoring the event prepares the advertising. When they are scheduled to do a show at a restaurant, the restaurant handles the advertising.

Adriana and Rick perform in a variety of settings. They do public shows at restaurants, as well as fund-raising events and private parties. They were even hired to perform their *Zoot Suit Swing Time Murders Show* at a wedding reception.

The Finances Involved. The establishments at which they perform also set the ticket price for a performance. Adriana used to handle ticket sales, but she is now happy to let the establishments take care of it. Tickets usually range from $35 to $50, depending on the type of event.

For a private event, the fee is usually $1,375, or $25 per person, whichever is the higher amount. There is a discounted price for senior citizens. Restaurants also receive a discount to offset the cost of advertising the event.

All of the actors have full-time professional careers outside of acting, so they do this work for the love of it. The actors are paid a set fee, plus any tips, and their meals are always included.

Adriana offers a "loyalty incentive," increasing an actor's pay after twelve performances. She is always willing to let any interested actors audition for the company.

Adriana and Rick don't do this work full-time, but for their own enjoyment. Rick is a respiratory therapist, and Adriana is a secretary and planning to attend school for stenography. They perform about one show every six weeks or so, and Adriana handles their bookings.

Getting Started. Aside from imagination and energy, there are a few things you will need to start your own mystery theater business. If you want to put on professional-quality shows, Adriana advises that you invest in a sound system. The system used by Grace Bentley Productions cost about $10,000, but Adriana considers it money well spent.

The actors all wear body mikes, which are important when performing in a large room. Without the microphones, audience members at the back of the room miss important clues and bits of information in the show. Invest in the best sound system you can afford, Adriana suggests, because it will only enhance the audience's appreciation of the show and add to the quality of your performances.

In addition, you will need costumes—Adriana and Rick now need costumes for three different shows, since they are all set in different decades. Sets, music, advertising, office space, and equipment are all factors in establishing your business. And don't forget that, if you won't be writing your own scripts, you will need to pay royalties.

Some Advice from Adriana. Adriana Rogers has a few tips for anyone interested in working in mystery theater. She loves her work, but she cautions that it has to be taken seriously: "It's really fun, but it's still work. You still have to maintain a professional attitude even if your character is kooky."

As a performer, you must be very mindful of your audience. Many people prefer to watch the show quietly and don't want to participate; some love to be involved in the action. Experience will tell you which people don't want to be pulled into the story; don't force them up onto the dance floor. There are always plenty of people who want to jump right in and have a good time.

MurderWatch Mystery Theater

Another company that combines love of mystery with the drama of theater is MurderWatch Mystery Theater. Connie and Jeffrey Gay produce, direct, and write a series of shows that they perform in Orlando, Florida.

After several years of performing in musical theater, Connie and Jeffrey wanted to try something new. They saw that mystery shows were becoming popular and decided to write their own material, add music, and get the audience involved in the action. They have been performing weekly at the Grosvenor Resort Hotel for more than ten years.

"Every Saturday night, guests get to play detective, and they also might become suspects," says Connie. "We make sure that there's activity in every section of the room. We make it so everyone sees something, no one sees everything, and everyone gets caught in the act." They have recently also begun performing at the Garden Eatery in St. Augustine.

The Finances Involved. When MurderWatch Mystery Theater began, Connie and Jeffrey realized it would be difficult to manage if they only took a cut of the sales, since attendance varied. As Connie says, "Some nights we'd get 150 people; some, only 80. But we still had to pay the same expenses. We agreed to charge a flat fee. The fee can vary from hotel to hotel. We pay the actors and buy our own equipment. We also have our own liability insurance." A ticket at the Grosvenor Hotel costs $39.95; at the Garden Eatery, $24.95

The actors, musicians, and technicians are all independent contractors. The company uses about thirty-five different actors, musicians, and technicians. There are six different shows, each using eight to ten performers.

Connie says that an advantage that she and Jeffrey have is their theater background and awareness of the business aspect of what they do. "Jeff worked for eight years in a bank, and . . . I worked eight years as a computer analyst. You can't organize yourself and a group of people, especially people with egos, if you don't have a solid business background.

"In the theater everyone becomes close and like family, and it's fun to be able to keep that atmosphere like we do, but it is a business and you can't lose sight of that fact. If you do, and you get lax, you can fail.

"We have our long-term goals, and we know where we're heading as a business. And the fun we have along the way is the fringe benefit. There's always a let's-put-on-a-show atmosphere, but we never lose sight of the bottom line."

Paranormal Investigation

Are you comfortable working outside what might be considered the norm? Are you unbothered by being doubted and challenged by the opportunity to prove a point? Do you have a sixth sense or a fascination with other-worldly matters? If you answered yes to these questions, then you might enjoy working as a paranormal investigator.

When it comes to the realm of the paranormal, people are usually divided into two distinct groups. There are the believers, those who cannot be shaken from their stand, and the nonbelievers, those who will never be convinced.

The strong beliefs of some, either for or against, have led to some interesting careers. There are not a great many job opportunities in this area, but a dedicated self-starter with the right combination of skill and determination could certainly earn some extra money in this field.

A Little History

Interest in psychic phenomena can be traced back to early times. The first modern organizations to investigate such phenomena were the British Society for Psychical Research, founded in 1881, and the American Society for Psychical Research, founded in 1885.

Much of the early investigation conducted by these two groups was unscientific and anecdotal in nature. J. B. Rhine, a psychologist at Duke University in Durham, North Carolina, wanted to change the approach and methods used. He began his work investigating parapsychology in 1927. In the course of his work, Rhine coined the term *extrasensory perception*. In 1935, Duke eventually allowed him to split from the psychology department and form the first parapsychological laboratory in the country. More than twenty years ago, the parapsychology department and Duke University parted ways, but those carrying on Rhine's work did not want to let it die. They soon formed the Institute for Parapsychology, which is also located in Durham.

The Controversy

The majority of scientists outside the field of parapsychology do not accept the existence of psychic phenomena. As a result, they do not accept the discipline of parapsychology. In scientific thinking, in order to study something, there has to be something tangible to study.

The harshest criticism leveled against parapsychologists is that of fraud. Rhine himself discovered that one of his researchers had been faking results, and the man was dismissed. Parapsychologists counter this charge by saying that they do well in policing their own ranks.

Another charge is that parapsychologists are not trained to tell whether a subject is committing fraud and thereby duping the researcher. Even amateur magicians have been known to fool investigators. Parapsychologists insist that this type of fraud happens only in an insignificant number of cases.

Another major criticism is that for phenomena such as extrasensory perception to be true, basic physical laws would have to be broken. To counter that, some parapsychologists believe that breakthroughs in particle physics may one day provide explanations for such phenomena. Others feel that paranormal activity operates outside the realm of science. Toward the end of his life, the great psychologist Carl Jung suggested that the deepest layers of the unconscious function independently of the laws of space, time, and causality, allowing for paranormal phenomena.

Other charges against parapsychology include shoddy experimental design, incorrect statistical interpretations, and misread data. A study in 1988, conducted by the National Research Council, maintained that no scientific research in the past 130 years had proven the existence of parapsychological phenomena. The council did, however, find anomalies that could not readily be explained in some experiments. Parapsychologists claim that the study was biased because the members of the research committee were nonbelievers.

Joe Nickell, Paranormal Investigator

Joe Nickell is one of the few paid paranormal investigators in the country. He's a staff member of the Committee for the Scientific Investigation of Claims of the Paranormal (CSICOP), which is based at the Center for Inquiry, a nonprofit international organization with headquarters in Amherst, New York. For many years he worked independently in this unusual field.

Joe has had an interesting and colorful career. He has worked as a private investigator, a professional stage magician at the Houdini Hall of Fame (under the stage names Janus the Magician and Mendell the Mentalist), a blackjack dealer, a riverboat manager, a newspaper stringer, a historical and literary investigator, and a writer of articles and books. He has also earned bachelor's, master's, and doctorate degrees, all in English literature, from the University of Kentucky at Lexington.

How Joe Got Started. While working at the Houdini Hall of Fame, Joe became interested in paranormal investigation through people he worked with. He thought that exposing psychics was interesting and exciting, and soon Joe had the opportunity to investigate a haunted house called Mackenzie House, a historic building in Toronto where various phenomena were occurring late at night. Caretakers heard footsteps on stairs when no one was there, among other unexplained sounds.

Joe discovered that the sounds were all illusions. "They were real sounds, but they were coming from the building next door. The buildings were only forty inches apart, and the other building had a staircase made of iron that ran parallel to the Mackenzie House stairway. Whenever anybody went up and down the stairs next door, it sounded as if it were coming from within the Mackenzie House. The interesting thing to me was that no one had figured this out for ten years."

A skeptic might, like Joe Nickell, want to see proof of paranormal claims. In Joe's case, his skepticism led him to conduct his own investigations. He was in the Yukon Territory working as a blackjack dealer and writing an occasional newspaper piece when he met a group of men claiming that they could use their dowsing wands to find gold. Joe challenged the men to prove their claim under control-test conditions, and they agreed. He put gold nuggets in some boxes padded with cotton. Other boxes contained fool's gold or nuts and bolts, and some were empty. The boxes were all put into a sack; even Joe didn't know which contained the real gold. Psychic ability would have been the only way any of the men could have known what was in each box, and, as Joe says, "Of course, they failed the test miserably." He ended up writing an article about the experiment.

Whenever Joe heard of an interesting claim, he investigated. He worked on a major investigation of the Shroud of Turin, disproving claims that the image on the shroud could not be duplicated. Joe proved that the image could indeed be duplicated using a simple process, and his results were published in several magazines.

Joe's work on the Shroud of Turin was noticed by the Committee for Scientific Investigation of Claims of the Paranormal (CSICOP). Founded by such distinguished thinkers as Paul Kurtz, Carl Sagan, and Isaac Asimov, CSICOP was established to investigate claims of the paranormal. The founders were responding to the sensationalism of paranormal claims on television and in the tabloids and wanted to form a society that could address the issue.

In Joe's words, "CSICOP was set up to investigate, not to dismiss out of hand—not to start out to debunk—but simply to investigate claims of the paranormal. And if that meant debunking, so be it."

Joe volunteered for years for CSICOP, and was hired full-time in 1995. "The center needed a detective, a magician, a writer, and a researcher, and by hiring me they got all of them in one." He describes himself as "a magic detective." While parapsychologists believe that there is some power of the mind to read people's thoughts or divine the future, they know that there is no scientific evidence for any of this.

Joe's investigations have revealed many claims to be false, whether due to poor research methodology or tricksters using sleight-of-hand. This is Joe's area of expertise.

In the Limelight. Joe has been a guest on several television shows, including "Larry King Live," "The Sally Jesse Raphael Show," "Maury," and "The Charles Grodin Show." He describes himself as "the token skeptic. They put on the believers, the UFO abductees, and so forth, and I get a minute at the end to say, 'Bah humbug.'" He has also been a consultant on "Unsolved Mysteries" many times.

Investigative Work. Unlike some less-scrupulous investigators, Joe and his colleagues use real methods, not tricks, to investigate claims. They interview people, search for evidence, and look for causes. They do not use machinery or gadgets, since there is no scientific evidence that such methods prove or disprove the paranormal.

Joe is most interested in the investigative aspect of his work and finds solving mysteries the most rewarding part of his job. He has even challenged himself by looking back through history for the solutions to long-ago puzzles, which keeps his skills sharp.

Some Advice from Joe. Joe Nickell has some advice for any self-starters interested in a career investigating the paranormal. He advises reading the literature, particularly the skeptical literature. "The believers will mislead you with phony stories. . . . the CSICOP journal, the *Skeptical Inquirer*, is a good starting point." The reputable journal publishes reviews of books and articles on the paranormal.

Contact information for CSICOP, as well as for the American Society for Psychical Research, is listed in Appendix A.

Joe adds that learning about magic can also be useful. It will help you to understand how people can be fooled and what the different tricks are.

Depending on the area you're most interested in, journalism, psychology, and astronomy would be helpful areas of study. Investigators rely on each other and share information, so collaboration is often essential, and knowledge of various disciplines is a plus.

To pursue a career, investigate phenomena, then turn the resulting material into articles for magazines or newspapers. A writer specializing in this area could make some money. Joe cautions, however, that "if you are really interested in being a freelance writer and making a buck, you need to be on the other side of the belief coin. You can sell a pro-ghost story far easier than you can sell one that debunks it. But if truth and honesty matter to you, you will not sell out. You will report fairly and thoroughly."

The Training You'll Need

There are few university programs in this country now devoted to training parapsychologists or their counterpart debunkers. You can contact CSICOP, listed in Appendix A, for additional information. You might also want to review some of the books suggested in Appendix B.

CHAPTER SIX

Freelance Writing

F reelance writing, which is the dream pursuit of many a self-starter, could easily be considered a service, but because it's such an extensive topic, it deserves an entire chapter.

Freelance writers can find satisfying and financially rewarding work in one of two broad categories: writing for publication and writing for others. Related careers, such as fiction writing and working as a literary agent, can also be rewarding and will be discussed later in this chapter.

Writing for Publication

Visit any bookstore or newsstand and you will see hundreds of publications covering a variety of topics—from sports and cars to fashion and parenting. There are also many you won't see there—the hundreds of trade journals and magazines written for businesses, industries, and professional workers in as many different careers.

These publications all offer information on diverse subjects to their equally diverse readers. They are filled with articles and profiles, interviews and editorials, letters and advice, as well as pages and pages of advertisements. But without writers there would be nothing but advertisements between their covers—and even those are produced by writers!

Whether you work for a magazine full-time or as an independent freelancer, you will discover there is no shortage of markets where you can find work or sell your articles.

Differences Between Staff Writers and Freelancers

A staff writer is employed full-time by a publication. She or he comes into work every day and receives article assignments to research and write or works with an editor to develop ideas.

A freelance writer works independently, in rented office space or in a home office. Most freelance writers plan and write articles and columns on their own and actively seek out new markets in which to place them.

Staff writers might have less freedom with what they choose to write, but they generally have more job security and always know when the next paycheck will arrive. Freelancers trade job security and regular pay for independence.

Both freelancers and those permanently employed must produce high-quality work. They both have editors to report to and deadlines to meet.

Different Kinds of Articles

Articles fall into two broad categories: those that educate and those that entertain. Here is just a small sampling of the topics magazine articles cover.

- art
- aviation
- business and finance
- careers
- child care
- computers
- contemporary culture
- entertainment
- food
- gardening
- general interest
- health

- hobbies
- humor
- military
- nature
- pets
- photography
- politics
- psychology and self-help
- retirement
- science
- sports
- travel

Although the subject matter can be very different, most magazine articles include many of the same elements. They all start with an interesting "hook," that first paragraph that grabs the reader's (and the editor's) attention. They use quotes from real people, mention important facts, and sometimes include amusing anecdotes or experiences.

Getting That First Article Published

Freelance writers don't need long, impressive resumes to sell their first articles. The writing will speak for itself.

Before starting, read as many magazines as you can, in particular those you would like to write for. It's never a good idea to send an article to a magazine you have never seen before. Being familiar with the different magazines will also help you come up with future article ideas.

Once you have decided what you want to write about, there are two ways you can go. You can write the entire article "on spec," sending it off to appropriate editors with the hope that they will like your topic. Or first you can write a query letter, a kind of miniproposal, to see if there is any interest in your idea. Query letters will save you the time of writing articles you might have difficulty selling. Only once you're given a definite assignment do you then proceed.

There are three important keys to keep in mind to get your articles published:

1. Make sure your writing is polished and that your article includes all the important elements.
2. Make sure your letter and manuscript are neatly typed and mistake free.
3. Make sure you are sending your article to the right publication. A magazine that features stories only on planning the perfect wedding will not be interested in your piece on ten tips for the perfect divorce.

You can find out about different magazines and the kind of material they prefer to publish in the market guides listed in Appendix B.

The Finances Involved

Most writers are thrilled to see their "byline," that is, their name on the page, giving them credit for the article. And to writers, nothing is more exciting than the finished product, getting to see their stories in print.

Getting a check or a salary for your efforts can be rewarding as well, but, sadly for new freelancers, the checks might not come often enough and are not always large enough to live on.

While staff writers are paid a regular salary (though generally not a very high one), a freelancer gets paid only when he or she sells an article. Fees could range from as low as $20 to $2,000 or more depending on the publication. But even with a high-paying magazine, writers often have to wait until their stories are published before they are paid. Because publishers work so far ahead, planning issues six months or more in advance, payment could be delayed from three months to a year or more.

To the freelancer's advantage, sometimes the same article can be sold to more than one magazine or newspaper. These "resales" help to increase a writer's income without adding greatly to the workload. And you can also be paid additional money if you provide your own photographs to illustrate your articles.

Landing a Regular Column

Once a freelancer has become established, he or she can often land regular assignments with the same editors. This might turn into a permanent column in a magazine or newspaper. A writer can even become syndicated, selling the same column to newspapers across the country.

Bob Haehle, Garden Writer

When Bob Haehle opens his daily mail, he's never quite sure what he'll receive. "This is the grimmer side of my job," Bob explains. "People send me dead leaves or bits of fruit and seeds. Sometimes I get squashed bugs. They have only three legs remaining and they were sent wrapped in plastic, so they're moldy and a terrible mess by the time I get them. You never know what's coming next."

Bob is not the victim of a harassment campaign; he writes a weekly question-and-answer format garden column for the Fort Lauderdale *Sun-Sentinel*, a newspaper with a circulation of more than three hundred thousand. "I've developed a following. Readers cut out the columns and save them in scrapbooks. It's nice to know you're helping people."

Bob answers all questions that are sent to him. "Sometimes I have to play detective to figure out what plants they're referring to; people use all sorts of different regional names. And with certain problems, I can refer to my own garden. I have a collection of one of this or one of that—from a landscape point of view it might not always flow together that well, but as a study tool and a research tool, to know what's going on at any given time of the year, it's great to have all these things in the yard."

Questions range from how to protect backyard citrus trees from disease to how to encourage blossoms from a bird-of-paradise. (For best results in the latter situation, Bob recommends allowing the family dog to help with the watering.)

"South Florida is a very special area," Bob says, "horticulturally different from the rest of the United States, with the exception of Hawaii. There really aren't a lot of gardening books dealing with all the conditions here. An incredible number of people move down here every year, but they're coming from different parts of the country and don't know what they're getting into. They may have gardened up north, but here you could almost literally say that conditions are 180 degrees different from the way they are in other locales. . . . There are so many differences."

In addition to his column, Bob also regularly writes articles for the paper covering topics from roses and seashore gardening to storm-damage control and the proper pruning of trees.

He also freelances for a variety of regional magazines in addition to working with Time-Life garden encyclopedias.

The reason for all the activity, besides his love of what he's doing, is that it's difficult to make a living at freelance garden writing alone.

The Finances Involved. "I make about $100 a week for the column, maybe $150 for articles," Bob notes. "I enjoy writing, but only more or less when I feel like doing it. Someone more ambitious than I could probably make a full-time career out of it. They could work full-time on the staff of a paper, for example, but that's too structured for me."

How Bob Got Started. Bob is overly modest about his background, which is more than impressive. He has a bachelor's degree in environmental design/landscape architecture from the University of Massachusetts and a master's degree in horticulture and botanic garden management from the University of Delaware.

He worked as an educational horticulturist at Brookside Gardens outside of Washington, D.C., giving lectures and putting out a newsletter, and later as director of the facility. He took classes in horticultural writing during his master's program and also cohosted a radio phone-in show called "Plant Talk."

"You don't necessarily have to have a horticultural background to be a garden writer," acknowledges Bob, "but it does help. You should have a good background in English and also have some interviewing skills for doing articles. It's also important to build up a good personal library of key reference books."

You can find Bob Haehle's column every Friday in the Fort Lauderdale *Sun-Sentinel.*

Writing for Others

There are many people, business owners or politicians, for example, who, because they do not have either the skill or the time, hire the services of professional writers to do their writing for them. As a freelancer working for clients like these, you can keep busy writing magazine ads, travel brochures, political speeches, or press releases. The possibilities are as endless as the number of clients you can develop.

If you have an interest in writing, a good command of English grammar, a grasp of the political process, or knowledge of sales and marketing techniques—or if you are willing to learn—then a career writing for others might be for you.

When you write for others, you might work in a client's or employer's office, or you may be able to work from home as a freelance writer. You will meet with your client or employer and listen to what he or she needs. Your project might be a brochure describing a resort hotel or a magazine ad to sell a new product.

You will then have to estimate the amount of time the job will take you and what additional expenses, such as photography or art work, you will have. When you have calculated your time and the cost, you then give an exact price to the client. Even if your estimate was short and it takes you more time than you had initially planned, you still have to stick by your initial quote.

You most likely will be working on your own, and this means that you have to be self-motivated and disciplined. The client will want the project finished by a certain date and will expect you to deliver on time. That could mean you're working weekends and nights as well as days to get the job done.

What the Work Involves

When you write for others, you could be involved in a variety of projects. Advertising copywriters write all the words for magazine ads as well as radio and television commercials. To describe a client's product or the services a business offers, copywriters prepare the copy for brochures or pamphlets. They write all the text for direct-mail packages, which are used to sell products or services through the mail, such as magazine subscriptions or memberships in a book club.

Ghostwriters write books for people who don't have the necessary skills to do it themselves. The client could be a famous person, such as a former president or a movie star, who has a story to tell but needs help doing it. Ghostwriters sometimes get credit for their writing (you might see "as told to" on the book jacket cover), but many times they remain anonymous, writing from behind the scenes.

Press secretaries work for government officials, actors and actresses, or big corporations that are concerned with relations with the press. They schedule public appearances and read prepared statements to reporters. They also write press releases that announce an event, a service, or a product. The press releases are sent to various newspapers and television and radio shows in the hopes of receiving some free publicity.

Speech writers work with politicians and other public figures, listening to what they want to say, then writing the speeches they will deliver. When you listen to the president on the television or see the mayor or governor speaking to a group of voters, it's a good bet that the speech was written by someone else.

Finding Clients

Many writers work for ad agencies, gaining experience and making contacts before striking out on their own. Others might start with just one client, a big corporation, for example, that will send enough work their way.

Through building a reputation of being good worker who delivers on time, a writer can receive recommendations from current clients that lead to new clients. Word of mouth is how most writers build up business.

The Finances Involved

In many careers, especially in the various areas of the writing profession, you'll hear the expression, "The work is its own reward." What that means is the money you make doing that work isn't particularly exciting.

But, in the case of writing for others, the money can be as rewarding as the work. Most people who write for others do it on a freelance basis. Although some charge a flat hourly rate, most charge by the project. It can be feast or famine starting out, but once you build a steady client base, your income can be very attractive.

There are a few writers who do earn a straight salary, such as press secretaries and writers who work for advertising agencies or public relations firms. Salaries in these positions can range anywhere from $25,000 a year for entry-level positions to more than $75,000 for experienced employees who have achieved a measure of success.

Table 6.1 shows you what freelancers generally charge for a few selected projects. Freelance writers work by the hour or on a per-project basis, depending on the type of work and the client.

TABLE 6.1. Wages for Freelance Writers

	HOURLY	PER PROJECT
Advertising copywriting	$20–$100	$200–$4,000
Book-jacket copywriting		$100–$600
Brochures	$20–$50	$200–$4,000
Business catalogs	$25–$40	$60–$75 per printed page
Direct-mail package		$1,500–$10,000
Encyclopedia articles		$60–$80 per 1,000 words
Ghostwriting	$25–$100	$400–$25,000 or 100% of the advance and 50% of the royalties
Greeting cards		$20–$200 per verse
Press kits		$500–$3,000
Press releases		$80–$300
Speech writing	$20–$75	$100–$5,000 (depending on the client)
Technical writing	$35–$75	$5 per page

Benefits of Freelancing

Independence is one of the pluses of writing for others, as freelancers will tell you. For some jobs or projects, you can do your work in a home office, delivering the project when it's finished. You choose the projects you want to work on, and you set your own salary or fees.

The downside is that you have to learn how to promote yourself and seek out clients. In the beginning, you might have to call strangers on the phone or knock on office doors looking for work.

When you do have work, you'll also have deadlines. This means that you'll have to deliver your work on time, often requiring you to continue writing nights and weekends.

And some writers have a hard time asking for money. They would love to leave the business end of things to someone else. But when you write for others, you have to wear all the different hats. It's up to you to set the fee, draw up the invoices, and bill the client. It's also up to you to collect from the client if he or she happens to be late or seems as if he or she might not pay at all.

Rosalind Sedacca, Advertising Copywriter

Rosalind Sedacca is a business communications strategist whose experience includes more than twenty years as an award-winning advertising copywriter. She has written advertising copy for brochures, magazine ads, and television commercials. Rosalind believes that it's important to always meet deadlines and to always give clients a little more than they're asking for. It's important that they feel they're getting their money's worth.

"I write ads for magazines, television and radio commercials, brochures, direct-mail packages, video scripts, newsletters, sales letters, and any other kind of material that needs to be written to help a company sell its product," explains Rosalind.

"When you write an ad, the first thing you have to know is what the purpose is. Then you want to understand who the market is, who will eventually be reading your writing. You have to understand the demographics—their age, their background, their sex, their income, their education level, and their interests.

"If I'm writing a print ad for a teenage audience, I'm going to write it a lot differently from an ad for mothers or engineers.

"I work in tandem with other creative people who are graphic designers. I do the writing, and the graphic designers take care of the layout and the art. We team up and brainstorm; the words alone don't work unless they're placed on the page in attractive ways.

"The goal is to get people to visit, to buy, to subscribe, or to join. The products I write copy for include computers, hotels and resorts such as Club Med, banks and real estate companies, car and appliance manufacturers, museums, magazines—all sorts of things."

One of the most interesting projects Rosalind has ever worked on is a new invention designed to detect counterfeit products. "There are so many forgeries in the world, it's become an international crisis. Unsuspecting buyers, thinking they are purchasing real Rolex watches or Reebok shoes, for example, might end up with very good fakes. Counterfeiters also print fake tickets for sporting events or theater shows, or fake money from countries around the world."

Rosalind's client is the inventor of a device that will help stop this problem. He has created a plastic decoder that, when placed over a plastic strip on the product, will show whether it's genuine or not. Manufacturers can travel to different flea markets and shops to check for fake products. When the device is in place, they'll be able to read the words, "Genuine Reeboks" or "Genuine Currency." If those words don't appear, the manufacturers will know their products have been copied.

"My job was to write a detailed brochure describing this new invention and to also help set up a promotional tour," says Rosalind. "My client will soon be making appearances on '20/20' and other similar television shows."

How Rosalind Got Started. "I got started out of college, wanting to work for *Vogue* magazine in the editorial department," Rosalind recalls. "I thought I wanted to work in the fashion world. I grew up in New York City, and I went to [*Vogue*'s] personnel department, but there weren't any openings. Instead, I was offered a position in advertising. I went to work as an assistant to the woman who was writing all the subscription letters, the ones you receive through the mail that offer you subscriptions to different magazines.

"A year later, she left the company, and I became creative director of circulation promotion for Condé Nast Publications, which owns many publications, including *Vogue, Glamour, Mademoiselle, House and Garden,* and *Bride's* magazines. It was a pretty cushy job for someone who was twenty-one years old. It inadvertently made me a direct-mail/advertising expert. I was with them for two years, then I left and moved into more general advertising for various advertising agencies in New York City, St. Louis, and Nashville. In 1984, I went out on my own, and I've been independent since then."

What the Work Is Like. "It's very stimulating and creative," states Rosalind. "I never get bored; no two days are ever the same. What I like best, and what also can be a challenge, is that one minute I'm writing about a hotel, and the next minute I'm writing about a computer, and then I'm turning around and writing about a bank or about shoes. Sometimes it's hard to change mental gears, to switch from one topic to another. It's the plus and the minus together.

"But I've got a perfect mix. Part of the week I'm in my home office working at the computer. I don't have to get dressed; no one sees me. I'm just on the phone a lot. The other part of the week I'm at meetings, either getting new clients or delivering my work, and then I'm dressed to the hilt, showing myself as a professional.

"The phone can take a lot of my time, and I have to wear many hats. I do my own accounting and taxes, filing, and all the administrative work, such as sending bills to clients. I'd much rather be writing, but in a small business you have to do everything.

"And when you start out, the finances can be tricky at first. Feast or famine. But now it's smoothed out for me; I've been in business for a long time."

Becoming a Novelist

Fiction writers are creative, imaginative people. After all, they have to be: they make up stories for a living. Whether writing short stories or full-length novels, fiction writers must be able to create imaginary characters and events and make them seem real to their readers.

Fiction writers have to be troublemakers, too, inventing all sorts of problems for their characters. They have to make their conversations and thoughts entertaining and fill their characters' lives with action. Finally, fiction writers have to be expert problem solvers, helping their heroes find satisfying solutions to their troubles by the end of the story.

If you love to read fiction and you find yourself stopping in the middle of a book and saying out loud, "I could do that better," then maybe you can.

The Writer's Life

Few new fiction writers have the luxury of working at their craft full-time—this applies to even the most dedicated of self-starters. Most need to maintain some other sort of employment to help pay the bills until they are able to support themselves through their writing. Because of this, ambitious writers use every spare minute they have to work on their books or stories. John Grisham, for example, wrote a good deal of *The Firm* on yellow legal pads while taking the train to and from work as a full-time attorney in a law firm.

Others get up an hour earlier, stay up an hour later, turn down invitations to parties or other social events, or let the housework go—whatever they can do to find the time to write.

Successful authors who support themselves through their writing treat it as a full-time job. Most report learning how to discipline themselves to put in a certain number of hours each day.

Every writer chooses a schedule that is comfortable for him or her. Some work in the early hours of the morning, take afternoon naps, and then go back to the computer in the evenings. Others write for eight or ten or twelve hours straight each day for a period of months until the book is finished. Still others might take years to complete one volume.

There is no set formula for how a writer should work. The only rule is that you have to write. Author James Clavell says that even if you write only one page every day for a year, at the end of that time you'll have 365 pages. And that's a good-sized book.

The Many Categories of Fiction

Next time you visit a bookstore, take note of where the different books are shelved and what the signs in each section say. Here are some of the different genres or categories you'll encounter, with a few of their subgenres also included.

- action/adventure
- children's
- fantasy
- general/mainstream
- horror
- literary
- mystery
  - cozy
  - crime
  - detective
  - police procedural
- romance
  - contemporary
  - gothic
  - historical
  - regencies
- science fiction
- suspense
  - psychological
  - thriller

- western
- young adult

Getting Your Novel Published

Writing a short story or a full-length novel is only half the battle. In addition to honing your skills as an expert storyteller, you also have to be a knowledgeable salesperson. That means you must learn which publishers you should approach and how to approach them. There are several market guides, mentioned in Appendix B, that tell you what categories of fiction different publishers buy. The guides also list magazines that purchase short stories. You may wish to check your own book collection to learn who publishes the books you read.

Once you've made a list of possible markets, you need to make sure your approach is appropriate. Your manuscript must be typed and double-spaced, with your name at the top of each page. There are several sources (also in Appendix B) that can give you the information you need to format your manuscript properly.

Before you send in your completed manuscript, you should write the editor a brief letter describing your project. Include a one-page synopsis, or summary, of your book's plot and the first three chapters of your book as a sample. Don't forget to enclose a self-addressed stamped envelope (SASE). The editor will use this to send you a reply. If the editor likes what he or she sees, you'll probably receive a request to send more.

Alternatively, you can look for an agent first, following the same steps you'd use to make your approach to a publisher. In this case, you are asking that the agent consider you as a possible client.

After the query letters and sample chapters are in the mail, many new writers just sit back and wait for responses. Smart writers put that manuscript out of mind and get to work on the next one. And the next one. And the next one. In the end, the key to getting published can be summed up in one word: persistence.

The Finances Involved

"Don't give up your day job just yet," is what the experts advise. Even if you manage to break in and sell your first novel, you should expect to receive only about $2,500 or $5,000.

The six-figure advances that some superstar authors receive are not the norm. Zebra Books senior editor John Scognamiglio says, "That kind of stuff, like with John Grisham, doesn't really have anything to do with the rest of us. There are 110,000 new titles a year, and there are only 15 on the New York Times Bestseller List at a time. Most of the rest of us are going to make a moderate income and do a civilized business if we work very, very hard. There's not that much room at the top. And there isn't much of a middle class in publishing. You either make a little bit of money, which the grand majority will do, or you make a lot."

If you do manage to land that first book contract, you will receive an advance against royalties. A royalty is a percentage, usually 6 percent to 10 percent, of the money your book earns in sales. The advance is paid half on signing the contract, half on delivery and acceptance of the manuscript.

But money is not the only reason writers write. For some, the profession is almost an obsession—a burning desire to put words to paper, to start a book and see it to its finish. They wouldn't be happy doing anything else.

Other perks include recognition and publicity, although some might view the attention as a downside. Many writers report that the nicest perk is being able to go to work in their bathrobes.

Joyce Sweeney, Young Adult Writer

Joyce Sweeney started sending her work to magazines and publishers when she was just eight years old. She sold her first book when she was eighteen. Now, eight books later, Joyce still loves writing about adolescents; it's the time of life that fascinates her most.

How Joyce Got Started. "I knew I wanted to be a writer all my life," she says. "I started writing when I was a kid, and it made sense to be writing about other kids. But I didn't even know that the young adult (YA) genre existed. I was very ignorant about the whole thing.

"I would look through magazines to find the editors' addresses and send them a poem or something. I was used to rejections by the time I was a teenager. I didn't really know what I was doing, but the whole process made me feel good.

"Later, I wrote to agents and sent them samples of my work. Miraculously, I found an agent to represent me. She submitted *Center Line* to more than thirty publishers. I was getting pretty nervous, but I knew it was a good book. Then Delacorte Press held a contest for people who had never been published, and I won first place. The prize was $5,000 and publication. All of my books have since been published by Delacorte.

"I write about whatever interests me at the moment. My readers are ten- to fourteen-year-olds. My book called *Shadow* is a ghost story, but it's also about sibling rivalry and domestic violence. Another book is an adventure story about four boys trapped in a cave. I've written about suicide and homosexuality, too."

The Difficulties Involved. "When I was a kid, YA novels were not that great," remembers Joyce. "They were formula books that I didn't associate with quality. Then I realized that this was a niche where you could write high-quality fiction, and it wasn't so tough to get published. For me, it was a nice way to be true to myself.

"But it does get more and more competitive every year. The series books are giving us a hard time. The bookstores tend to buy the Baby-Sitter's Club and nothing else. If you are writing ordinary mainstream books, it's getting harder and harder.

"Also, I find it a little difficult to market myself, at least locally. If I go to a children's event, the kids there are too young for my books. If I go to an event with adult authors, no one there is really interested.

"And just being a writer is a constant struggle. It's difficult to write. It's difficult to keep writing. You know you could make more money in advertising.

"I've started books and found out that they were going nowhere and had to throw them out. I haven't had too many bad reviews, but I've had books that I thought were great that didn't sell that well. My second book, for example. There are ups and downs all the time.

"A big thing that happens to me a lot, though it doesn't sound much like a downside, is that I get approached by the movie industry to have my books made into feature films or television movies. But it never quite happens. They just get dropped.

"It's not a steady, calm sort of work. There's the unpredictability of sales and the market, the unpredictability of whether I'm writing something good at a given moment. I'm never sure if the next book will be okay, as good as the one before it."

On the Plus Side. "I think children are a more appreciative audience than adults," Joyce notes. "I go to schools, and I find I have real fans out there. They're excited and enthusiastic; they write letters to me. I can really see that I'm having an effect. I think back to when I was a kid, and I know that the books they read at that age make a huge difference. Books can change their whole lives or influence them this way or that way. It's exciting to be able to touch someone at that particular age.

"I never get tired of that. This is where I belong."

Some Advice from Joyce. "Read as much as you possibly can, and read the authors you would like to be like. Try to pick up as much as you can about writing that way," recommends Joyce. "Find out if there are any creative writing classes or programs available to you and enroll.

"And no matter how young you are, you should start to send your writing out, just for the practice and to get used to rejection slips."

Self-Publishing

For those writers whose books don't meet conventional publishing criteria—the topic or the audience are too narrow to make marketing the book cost-effective, for example—and who feel they can reach their audience by themselves, self-publishing might be the route to take.

The self-publisher sets up his or her own publishing company and controls every facet of production, promotion, and distribution. The financial outlay is the complete responsibility of the self-publisher. But in return, all profits, if there are any, go to the self-publisher.

Undertaking a self-publishing book project is a big step. It involves a lot of time and money, and the self-publisher needs to have a variety of skills in addition to writing ability. With self-publishing, marketing and promotional expertise are more important than being able to write.

The Finances Involved

Depending on how many copies of a book you print, the outlay could be anywhere from $5,000 to $15,000. When deciding how much to charge for your book, you need to remember that, unless you have a ready-made retail audience for the book, most of your sales will go to distributors, libraries, or bookstores. For those markets you will receive only 40 percent to 60 percent of the retail cost of your book.

Two Pitfalls to Avoid

1. **Don't overprint.** Your first run should be no more than two thousand copies. See if there's a market for your work before you fill up your living room or garage with cartons of books.
2. **Don't self-publish fiction.** Self-published books can be very difficult to sell—with fiction it borders on the impossible. Most self-published books carry an automatic

stigma: why wasn't it good enough for a legitimate publisher to take on? Some nonfiction books can avoid that stigma; most fiction can't.

Tom Bernardin, Author and Self-Publisher

Tom Bernardin worked as a seasonal employee for the National Park Service at Ellis Island for three years.

"Ellis Island is part of the Statue of Liberty National Monument," Tom explains. "They're two separate islands, but they're right beside each other.

"I had originally hoped to land a job on the maintenance staff at the Statue of Liberty. I wanted to cut grass. The woman who interviewed me and later became my boss took a look at my application and saw that I had a college degree and was a teacher of English as a second language to recent immigrants. She wanted me on her interpretive staff at Ellis Island. I was aware of the position, but at the time I'd had my public speaking experience only from teaching and I was a bit nervous. Still, I just knew that I'd like it. I'd always been interested in Ellis Island. It's so loaded with history. It opened in 1975 for visitors, and I had hoped to be on the first tour boat, but I was teaching that day.

"I took the job and had absolutely no regrets. The best part of my job was having access to Ellis Island and becoming a part of its history, making the public aware of how important it was, tapping into the emotions visitors brought with them."

Although it has been two decades since Tom Bernardin left his job at Ellis Island, the monument is still very much with him. In 1981 Tom developed a slide lecture called "Ellis Island: The Golden Door," and in 1991 he self-published his book, *The Ellis Island Immigrant Cookbook*. As well as recipes contributed by immigrants and their descendants, the pages are filled with heartwarming, and at times heart-wrenching, accounts of the Ellis Island experience.

Tom had two ready-made markets when he undertook to compile his book: the gift shops at both the Statue of Liberty and Ellis

Island. Tom also regularly tours the country speaking to groups about the rich history of Ellis Island. To date he has sold more than thirty thousand copies of his book.

Literary Agents

Perhaps you'd prefer to be on the other side of the desk, so to speak, helping writers get published, rather than writing yourself. If so, a career as a literary agent might be for you.

The Role of the Literary Agent

Literary agents act as go-betweens for writers and editors. It can be difficult, if not impossible, to get a book published without an agent, and most publishers won't even consider manuscripts unless agents submit them. An agent is expected to be familiar with the different kinds of books publishers prefer to take on in order to help writers avoid the pitfalls of sending a book to an inappropriate publisher.

An agent spends his or her time reading manuscripts, choosing which ones to work with, and then trying to sell them to publishers. Agents free a writer to concentrate on writing instead of marketing. The agent's job is to find the right publishing house for a client's work and, once successful, to negotiate the best financial deal for the writer. Agents also handle film rights for feature or television movies as well as foreign rights, selling books to publishers overseas.

How Literary Agencies Are Structured

Some literary agents choose to work on their own, with little more than secretarial assistance. They rent space in office buildings or work from home. Other agents prefer to work within literary agencies, either as owners or as associates. They can still function independently, choosing the writers and book projects they want to work with. Usually, agents working in agencies must contribute a percentage of their income to cover office operating expenses.

Training for Agents

Most agents have at least a bachelor's degree, although not necessarily in English. Any liberal arts or humanities major, in addition to writing and literature courses, will provide the necessary background. It is also helpful to be familiar with publishing law and contracts and to know how to type and use a computer.

Most skills can be learned through on-the-job experience, but, as with writers, agents should also be avid readers.

The Finances Involved

Agents must sell their clients' manuscripts to publishers in order to earn any income. Agents generally work on a commission basis, usually 10 percent to 15 percent of the money the writer earns. If an agent has a lot of market savvy, carefully chooses which manuscripts to represent, and has success bargaining for big advances and royalty percentages, he or she can make a very good living, often much more than the editors to whom he or she is selling.

The downside for agents is that the marketplace is fickle. Fads come and go, and publishing houses merge and often decrease the number of books they print. In a bad year, an agent may have to struggle to make a living.

Nancy Yost, Literary Agent

Nancy Yost started as a contract editor at Random House, then moved to Avon Books as an editor from 1986 to 1990. She became a full-time agent at Lowenstein Associates in New York. Today, she is a partner in the agency, now called Lowenstein-Yost Associates. It represents more than 150 authors of fiction and nonfiction.

"Publishing houses are organized by lists—they have certain kinds of books they're good at, and they have certain kinds of books they don't do," says Nancy.

"For example, Avon is very good with romances, very good with original mysteries, and they have great science fiction and fantasy editors. But if you ever wanted to work with a big picture book or a cookbook, you couldn't. You were limited by the list. It seemed to me that if I became an agent, I'd be able to play in everyone's backyard instead of just one."

Another plus is the financial aspect. As Nancy says, "The money is better, of course; the more you sell, the more you earn. And you only work with the people you want to work with. Even in the best of publishing houses you have salespeople, marketing people, production people who are many times at odds with your vision of a book or your enthusiasm for a book. The only limit on my enthusiasm now is what I think the market can do. If one publisher doesn't like it, I can go to six others—or twenty others—until I sell it or until I've been beaten down and realize I'm not going to be able to sell it."

A successful literary agent keeps a very full schedule. As a full-time agent, Nancy handles up to fifty clients at a time. This is not quite as daunting as it may seem because not all of them are producing books simultaneously. If each writer produces one or two books a year, the schedule is more manageable.

Nancy describes her approach to her work: "I receive a lot of submissions every week—query letters and complete manuscripts. How I approach my submissions is in the nature of triage. The ones that are going to die, I have to reject right away; the ones that I'm really excited about, I ask to see more of right away. The ones that look as if there might be something there but that don't really stand out tend to sit the longest. The converse of that is being sent something that's really good at a time when I'm too busy with other commitments. Sometimes I have trouble finding a chunk of time to devote to it."

When Nancy has a good submission, she telephones editors before sending it to them. This gives her the opportunity to get a feel for whether they are interested, and it also allows her to express her own enthusiasm for the work.

The hard part, for Nancy, is rejecting a manuscript. "Part of me always cringes when I have to reject a manuscript I have no interest in. But if I'm not the right person to handle it, it's better the writer knows right away.

"And sometimes there's a problem with rude writers and messy manuscripts. Once in a while an attitude comes through that puts you off."

For More Information

Books and professional associations of interest to writers and potential agents are listed in Appendixes A and B.

CHAPTER SEVEN

Organizations and Cooperative Enterprises

Not only are you a self-starter, you're an organized one. You make to-do lists for all your activities, and you keep track of them and check off items as they are completed. You have a knack for pulling people together for an event or special occasion. If a party needs to be planned and catered, a seminar organized, a luncheon meeting put together, you're the person at the helm, controlling all the various elements. And you enjoy doing it.

You pay attention to details, you can juggle different tasks at the same time, and, as the event draw nears, you not only watch everything fall into place, you make sure it does.

What can a self-starter do with these valuable skills? Many entrepreneurs with similar skills channel their abilities into organizing some of the following events:

- seminars
- workshops
- conventions
- conferences
- weddings
- parties
- associations
- collectives

- clubs
- speakers' bureaus

How to Get Started

The self-employed organizer must first see a need or, when no apparent need exists, develop one. If you're a writer, you can organize seminars; if you're a plant lover, you can arrange garden exhibitions; if you're a photographer, you can put on a community photography competition.

You can also contact existing groups—writers' associations, historical societies, chambers of commerce, to name just a few—and let them know of your services.

Each event or organization has its own particular requirements. Here are some of the details an organizer might have to attend to:

- raising financing
- arranging for a venue, such as a conference hall, hotel ballroom, or school gym
- hiring speakers or entertainment
- catering refreshments
- designing, writing, printing, and distributing promotional material
- renting equipment or furnishings
- keeping track of registrations or guest lists
- sending invitations and confirmation letters
- allocating seating
- arranging for accommodations
- coordinating transportation

This chapter provides a few examples of successful projects for organizers.

Starting an Association

Do you have an avid interest or hobby or an unusual occupation for which there seems to be little professional support, especially in your specific location? If so, you can start your own membership organization or professional association.

Dana Cassell, Association Organizer

Dana Cassell is a freelance writer. Since 1971, more than two thousand of her articles have appeared in two hundred publications, including consumer, business, and trade magazines. Dana has provided editorial services to dozens of clients, from individuals to corporations, including editing, newsletter production, and ad copywriting. She is the editor for the Dream Jobs to Go series at Intellectua.com. She is also director and founder of Florida Freelance Writers Association and Cassell Network of Writers (CNW).

Dana describes the impetus for beginning her association: "After working for almost ten years building up a client base, getting to know editors and other writers I met at conferences, I realized that these two groups sometimes had difficulty finding each other. That's how the idea for CNW was born.

"With the goal in mind to act as a link between editors and writers and to provide information to writers to enable them to be more successful, I tested the market to see what the interest level was. After a positive response to my initial mailing, I did a bigger mailing. I attracted three hundred members the first year.

"CNW was a natural outgrowth of that basic profession of being an independent writer. I always thought I would keep writing and that CNW would be just a sideline. But it grew and grew and took over, becoming the main focus.

"I expect I will always write," she continues. "When I 'retire,' I will just divest myself of the other parts of the business."

The Ups and Downs. For Dana Cassell, the independence of being self-employed makes it all worthwhile. As she says, "I love the freedom of being my own boss, the excuse to talk to anybody about anything while doing research, the continual use of books and libraries and magazines, the ability to work at home—which I love—seeing my byline (one never gets tired of that), and the satisfaction that the information I communicate via workshops and seminars has helped a writer become successful.

"But as satisfying as that is, I'm not sure it quite equals what it's like to come up with an idea for an article or book, follow it through, and have someone else publish it with your name on it."

On the other hand, Dana's schedule is very busy, and the work doesn't take a break, even when she does. "When I do take time off, the work continues to pile up and deadlines loom closer, so I have to work twice as hard when I return—which is the major reason I don't take lengthy vacations.

"There's also the financial insecurity. We all dream of a bestseller. I'd probably still work as hard and as long, but it would be nice to eliminate the will-enough-money-come-in-this-week-to-pay-the-bills syndrome.

"And because CNW has so many members, I have less time to write now."

How Dana Got Started. Dana's experience on her high school newspaper helped her get a job on a small weekly paper. She began reading the editor's copies of *Writer's Digest* and realized that she could write magazine articles. As she says, "It opened a whole new world for me.

"After several years of studying and practicing, I became a real, published freelance writer and discovered that this was what I was happiest doing. I could never get completely away from it, even when I tried to."

What CNW Is. Cassell Network of Writers is a membership organization of writers wanting to learn more about their craft, how to get their work published more regularly, and how to manage the business side of freelancing. Dana produces a newsletter each month packed with such information as writing and business tips, market listings for articles, contests for writers, and a calendar of events such as seminars and workshops.

She has organized all-day seminars and three- and four-day statewide writers' conferences, bringing in speakers—published authors, editors, and agents—from all over the country. She also runs a member referral service, connecting freelancers with anyone who requires the services of a writer.

Starting a Collective

Moosewood Restaurant in Ithaca, New York, opened its doors in 1973 as a collectively run vegetarian dining establishment. Part of the counterculture at the time, Moosewood workers were early adherents to the now-popular philosophy that food can be healthful and taste good at the same time. They also felt that the workplace should be a fun place to be, with all business decisions made jointly. At present, eighteen women and men rotate through the jobs necessary to make the restaurant run, planning menus, setting long-term goals—and washing pots. Their ranks are bolstered by about half a dozen employees. Most of the Moosewood collective members have worked together for more than ten years, several since the restaurant's early days.

Moosewood was at first known only locally. Now, two decades and several highly acclaimed cookbooks later, Moosewood's reputation for serving fine food in a friendly atmosphere has spread nationally. And the collective has not lost sight of its original philosophy. Moosewood is still owned and run collectively and still serves quality meals at reasonable prices.

David Hirsch, Chef and Cookbook Author

David Hirsch joined the Moosewood collective in 1976. He started as a waiter/busboy but soon took on the responsibilities of chef and menu planner. He is also the author of *The Moosewood Restaurant Kitchen Garden* and coauthor, with other collective members, of all six Moosewood cookbooks: *New Recipes from the Moosewood Restaurant, Sundays at Moosewood Restaurant, Moosewood Restaurant Cooks at Home, Moosewood Restaurant Cooks for a Crowd, Moosewood Restaurant Low-Fat Favorites,* and *Moosewood Restaurant's Book of Desserts.*

Making a Collective Work. Collectives have come and gone over the years. There are many elements that go into making one work. If this is a career path that intrigues you, these tips from David Hirsch can point you in the right direction. "To start a successful collective, just like with any business, you first must judge the need, do some market research. Are people clamoring for this business to serve them?"

David stresses the importance of finances in establishing a collective. He warns that most banks are unlikely to lend money to a business without any collateral. It might be easier for individual members, or their backers, to obtain loans based on their personal collateral. Many people take second mortgages on their homes, for example.

"With Moosewood, an enormous amount of money wasn't necessary," says David. "We started with a small space and bought some secondhand equipment."

David also advises that someone involved in the project should have some business background. If no one does, hiring a professional is a good idea. It is wise to have someone with the expertise to protect your investment.

The restaurant business has its own set of demands, and you must be able to work under pressure in order to be successful, according to David. He credits Moosewood's success with its members' dedication to finding interesting international recipes that continue to please customers.

He also cites the staff's ability to work well together. As David describes it, "In a worker/manager situation, you need to be somehow connected to other people who have similar interests. You can't do it yourself; you need good support, a network of people you trust. We didn't put an ad in the paper looking for collective members. Moosewood is unique, a network of connected friends and acquaintances that grew in a fairly organic way."

David also talks of the need to keep the collective fresh and interesting. "Once you are involved, try to create situations that can expand your interest in whatever you want to do so it doesn't get stale. Look for something that really excites you, interests you. You have to be comfortable with it. If you find yourself watching the clock wishing you were out of there, then you probably should be out of there.

"Being a part of a collective involves commitment. With a more traditional job, you can just go home at the end of the day. With a collective, there are meetings to attend and responsibilities to share. You have to be willing to do that."

Getting a Foot in the Door. "We occasionally take on new members," says David. "To be a part of Moosewood, we'd have to see a resume, but we tend to hire people we can interview on a personal basis. We work very closely together in a small space."

Anyone interested in joining Moosewood should write to the collective. If the members like the letter and resume, the applicant is invited to Ithaca for an interview. David suggests that potential applicants take some cooking courses, particularly in vegetarian cuisine. These can usually be found at select culinary institutes, community colleges, and adult education programs.

No one at Moosewood becomes a star right away. New members work with senior staff to learn the ropes and feel comfortable with the restaurant's operation. A new chef might start out as an extra cook on a shift before eventually working on his or her own.

How David Got Started. David earned his bachelor of architecture degree in 1968 at City College of New York. He worked in various architectural firms for a few years before moving to

Ithaca. "My desire to leave the city and join the back-to-the-land movement brought me to Ithaca in 1972," he recalls. "I spent a couple of years building a house in the country. Then, to earn some money, I got a job as a cook for a couple of different fraternities at Cornell University. I could have summers off and could devote time to other pursuits. My interest in architecture was replaced with my love of the earth, gardening, hiking, and the out-of-doors.

"But I discovered I also loved to cook. It's fun and direct; the results are immediate."

David became involved with Moosewood during the collective's third year. Although he wasn't looking for a long-term career, he found that he was working with people who shared his values, and that made a big difference.

David's Duties at Moosewood. David divides his time among cooking, planning menus, ordering food and supplies, testing recipes for the books, writing, attending meetings, and occasionally waiting on tables.

Because of the Moosewood cookbooks, David is occasionally involved in book promotions, attending local book signings and appearing on television and radio shows. He also does some catering and consulting and teaches hands-on cooking workshops.

The Finances Involved. Because of the nature of the collective, the members of Moosewood are less concerned with fortune than they are with finding satisfaction in their work. As David notes, "With so many people sharing dividends, income gets watered down, even with a large book advance."

David readily states that the financial rewards of working in a restaurant collective are not great. Entry-level salaries usually start somewhere in the teens. After three or four years' experience, a member could earn $25,000 or so, depending on how many hours a week he or she chooses to work.

"The reasons to be in our collective have to be heartfelt," David believes. "Rewards could be more financial in another type of collective or venture, but not necessarily so. It depends on the market, where you are, and what service or product you provide."

The Ups and Downs. David felt comfortable at Moosewood right from the start. As he recalls, "It felt different to me from any other job. There's no hierarchy; you're working with peers. There are built-in checks and balances and no authority figures to say, 'You have to do it this way because I say so.' Everyone's on equal ground."

This equality fosters a very supportive atmosphere, rather than the competitiveness often found in other establishments. Without a hierarchy, there is much more equanimity. As David says, "You go in, make the food, and people appreciate it. This is something I can care about. I feel good about what I'm doing."

Another plus is the hours. While most traditional restaurant owners often work sixty to seventy hours a week, members of a collective can work fewer hours if they choose to. Since everyone is an owner, the work is shared on a much more equitable basis than in a traditional setting.

Of course, there are some negatives. "What I like least is dealing with the push and pull from all the different directions, the different people," admits David. "The collective process, working toward consensus, can be frustrating at times."

Finger Lakes Organic Growers Cooperative

Finger Lakes Organic Growers is a cooperative enterprise with fifteen active member farms spread across Upstate New York. Together these farms comprise 1,000 acres of farms and woodlands, with 180 acres in fruit and vegetable production and 85 acres in organic grains.

The aim of the member farms is to grow all their crops organically without the use of any chemical pesticides or fertilizers. The farmers are committed to sustainable agriculture, meaning they employ farming methods that benefit the environment—the soil gets richer and the general ecology is preserved.

Carol Stull, Grower

Carol Stull was a founding member of the Finger Lakes Organic Growers Cooperative. Unfortunately, since generously sharing information about the cooperative, Carol has died. Her insights and observations remain a valuable legacy, along with her hope that they would inspire like-minded self-starters to pursue their dreams.

Carol described the cooperative's beginning in 1986: "It actually started under the black locust tree in my backyard. There had been a group of growers, about six of us, who had been meeting and talking about how running around and trying to sell everything ourselves was a hassle. Several of our regular customers would buy one thing from someone, but if they ran out, they'd go to someone else. So our thinking was that if we could go together it would be more expeditious."

After a year of discussion, the group began its enterprise. The members applied for a grant from New York State Department of Agriculture and Markets, which had federal funds to dispense for state grants. They received $15,000, which they used as start-up money for the cooperative.

Initial expenditures included setting up a computer program and renting a truck for deliveries. The market manager worked out of her home, and the co-op used a member's farm for storage space instead of renting a warehouse. The initial operation was low budget, but the group did purchase office supplies and hire an artist to design a logo.

As Carol described it, each member owns a farm. The members decided right away that they would not compete with one another in the marketplace, so they set up a personnel committee to coordinate efforts. "We each gave up all our wholesale markets to the co-op. It used to cost us at least a quarter of our time to do the selling, and that really wasn't enough to do it right. So we've changed that now, and the manager takes care of all of that."

Carol's Individual Farm. Carol and her husband bought their land in Ithaca, New York, in 1985.

"Our business (CRS Growers) was only a year old when we started the cooperative. Before that we used to market our produce directly at farmers' markets. We were small, just learning to go from packets to pounds. You buy a packet of seeds for a small home garden, but when you're growing commercially you buy seeds by the pound.

"We have sixty-five acres and farm about ten acres of it. We grow all of the standard vegetables, except corn. We have a problem with deer.

"One of the reasons I like doing this is that I can grow any weird thing I want. That was one of our entries into the wholesale restaurant market. I can grow edible flowers or unusual cherry tomatoes that other people don't grow. We also grow a lot of herbs—seven or eight different basils, for example."

The Stulls' employee roster fluctuates. They hire students in the summer to help with the planting and picking. In Carol's opinion, "It's a lot easier if you have several thousand tomato plants and six or eight people to chat with as you're picking. Then it can be fun work. By yourself it's a lot harder."

Carol did all the planning for the farm. Since it grows so many different crops, it is important to know where they're going to go. The farm is operated on a three-year rotation, which means workers don't plant crops from the same family in the same place in the field for three years.

The farm has three greenhouses; in the winter salad greens are grown for the hotel school at Cornell University in Ithaca. The produce is also sold at the local farmer's market on Saturdays, and there is a roadside stand on the property. As Carol said, "When you have more cherry tomatoes than you absolutely know what to do with, you look at every market available."

The Difficulties of Farming. Unforeseen circumstances can take a toll on even the most careful planning, and a farmer must be able to adapt to change. As Carol said, "There's a lot of planning and a lot of adjusting to your planning if things don't work out— whether it's the weather that doesn't cooperate or the equipment breaks down or someone doesn't show up or things grow faster or slower than you thought they would. You spend a lot of time figuring out what you're doing. We have 187 different food products and a wide line of perennials and herb plants, and that's a lot going on."

Carol's Background. Carol was trained as a clinical chemist with a biology background and worked for eighteen years as a hospital chemist. She earned her bachelor's degree at the University of Illinois and her master's at Baylor University in Texas. Although she grew up in suburban Evanston, Illinois, there's been a farm in her family since her great-grandfather's time.

Carol spoke of her love for farming. "We have a very inspiring view. Our farm sits on top of a hill overlooking twenty miles of Cayuga Lake. If you're feeling a little down in the morning, the view will perk you up. But what I like most is the fascination of seeing a little seedling transfer into something big, watching the flowers open up. Then seeing the fruits of your labor when you go out and start harvesting. The little plants you transplanted are now ready to be eaten or sold or whatever you're going to do with them. It's a thrill."

The Finances Involved. Income for farmers can vary from year to year. Food prices fluctuate from week to week and are affected by the weather and other factors that influence the demand for certain products. The size and type of farm also affects income.

Generally, large farms produce more income than smaller operations. The exception to that generalization are specialty farms that produce small amounts of high-value horticultural and fruit products.

According to the U.S. Department of Labor, full-time, salaried farm managers had median weekly earnings of $542 in 2000. The middle half earned between $221 and $655. The highest-paid 10 percent earned more than $756, and the lowest-paid 10 percent earned less than $187.

Seasonal farm workers generally earn between minimum wage and $10 an hour.

Farmers who are part of growers' cooperatives earn different amounts depending on the size of the property and what kind of year they had. The earnings could range from just a few thousand dollars to as much as $60,000 in gross sales for smaller farms and considerably more for larger tracts.

As Carol Stull said, "People don't realize how much it costs to grow food. I'm still selling things at the same price I was ten years ago because that's what people expect to pay. But ten years ago the minimum wage was lower; now it's gone up, and I pay workman's compensation and social security, too.

"It's what I do for a living, but my husband also has a full-time job outside the farm. I wouldn't be able to do this at this level if it were just me. As you pay off your equipment and mortgage, you have a little more left over for your own salary, but it's not easy."

Because the work for some farmers and managers is seasonal, and the income fluctuates so, many growers take second jobs during the off months.

Professional Associations

The following organizations can provide additional information about the various careers discussed throughout this book.

Bed-and-Breakfasts

Professional Association of Innkeepers International
P.O. Box 90710
Santa Barbara, CA 93190
www.paii.org

Floral Industry

American Floral Art School
529 South Wabash Avenue, #600
Chicago, IL 60605

American Floral Endowment
11 Glen-Ed Professional Park
Glen Carbon, IL 62034
www.endowment.org

American Institute of Floral Designers
720 Light Street
Baltimore, MD 21230
www.aifd.org

Canadian Academy of Floral Art
355 Elmira Road North, Unit 103
Guelph, ON N1K 1S5
Canada
www.cafachat.com

Society of American Florists
1601 Duke Street
Alexandria, VA 22314
www.aboutflowers.com

Art and Antiques Appraisal

American Society of Appraisers
555 Herndon Parkway, Suite 125
Herndon, VA 20170
www.appraisers.org

Canadian Personal Property Appraisers Group
1881 Scanlan Street
London, ON N5W 6C3
Canada
www.cppag.com

The Appraisal Foundation
1029 Vermont Avenue NW, Suite 900
Washington, DC 20005
www.appraisalfoundation.org

Auctioneering

Auctioneers Association of Canada
5240 - 1A Street SE, Suite 100
Calgary, AB T2H 1J1
Canada
www.auctioneerscanada.com

Missouri Auction School
13735 Riverport Drive
Earth City, MO 63045
www.auctionschool.com

National Auctioneers Association
8880 Ballentine
Overland Park, KS 66214
www.auctioneers.org

Hairstyling and Cosmetology

National Accrediting Commission of Cosmetology Arts and
    Sciences
4401 Ford Avenue, Suite 1300
Alexandria, VA 22302
www.naccas.org

Accrediting Commission of Career Schools/Colleges of
    Technology
2101 Wilson Boulevard, Suite 302
Arlington, VA 22201
www.accsct.org

National Cosmetology Association
401 North Michigan Avenue, Suite 2200
Chicago, IL 60611
www.salonprofessionals.org

Personal Trainers

American College of Sports Medicine (ACSM)
401 West Michigan Street
Indianapolis, IN 46202
www.acsm.org

American Council on Exercise (ACE)
4851 Paramount Drive
San Diego, CA 92123
www.acefitness.org

Canadian Fitness and Lifestyle Research Institute
201-185 Somerset Street West
Ottawa, ON K2P 0J2
Canada
www.cflri.ca

Genealogy

Association of Professional Genealogists
P.O. Box 350998
Westminster, CO 80035
www.apgen.org

Board for Certification of Genealogists
P.O. Box 14291
Washington, DC 20044
www.bcgcertification.org

Federation of Genealogical Societies
P.O. Box 200940
Austin, TX 78720
www.fgs.org

Family History Library
Church of Jesus Christ of Latter-Day Saints
35 Northwest Temple Street
Salt Lake City, UT 84150
www.familysearch.org

National Genealogical Society
4527 Seventeenth Street North
Arlington, VA 22207
www.ngsgenealogy.org

Arborists

International Society of Arboriculture
1400 West Anthony Drive
Champaign, IL 61821
www.isa-arbor.com

Paranormal Investigation

American Society for Psychical Research
5 West Seventy-Third Street
New York, NY 10023
www.aspr.com

Committee for the Scientific Investigation of Claims of the
  Paranormal (CSICOP)
Center for Inquiry
P.O. Box 703
Amherst, NY 14226
www.csicop.org

Freelance Writing and Literary Agents

American Society of Journalists and Authors
1501 Broadway, Suite 302
New York, NY 10036
www.asja.org

Association of Authors Representatives (AAR)
P.O. Box 237201
Ansonia Station
New York, NY 10003
www.aar-online.org

Literary Market Place
Information Today, Inc.
143 Old Marlton Pike
Medford, NJ 08055
www.literarymarketplace.com

Farming and Collective Enterprises

American Farmland Trust
1200 Eighteenth Street NW, Suite 800
Washington, DC 20036
www.farmland.org

National Family Farm Coalition
110 Maryland Avenue NE, Suite 307
Washington, DC 20002
www.nffc.net

Northeast Organic Farming Association (NOFA)
P.O. Box 21
South Butler, NY 13154
www.nofa.org

Recommended Reading

The following are resources that will provide further information to help you make a decision about your entrepreneurial career.

Bed-and-Breakfasts

Cozzens, Michele VanOrt. *I'm Living Your Dream Life: The Story of a Northwoods Resort Owner*. Indian Wells, CA: McKenna Publishing Group, 2002.

Davies, Mary E. *So . . . You Want to Be an Innkeeper*. San Francisco: Chronicle Books, 1996.

Floral Industry

Camenson, Blythe. *Careers for Plant Lovers and Other Green-Thumb Types*, 2nd Edition. Chicago, IL: VGM Career Books, 2004.

deJong-Stout, Alisa A. *A Master Guide to the Art of Floral Design*. Portland, OR: Timber Press, 2002.

Scace, Pat Diehl. *The Floral Artist's Guide*. Clifton Park, NY: Delmar Learning, 2001.

Genealogy

Board for Certification of Genealogists. *The BCG Genealogical Standards Manual*. Orem, UT: Ancestry, 2000.

Eales, Anne Bruner, and Robert M. Kvasnicka, eds. *Guide to Genealogical Research in the National Archives of the United States*, 3rd Edition. Washington, D.C.: National Archives and Records Administration, 2000.

Greenwood, Val D. *The Researcher's Guide to American Genealogy*, 3rd Edition. Baltimore: Genealogical Publishing Co., 2000.

Mills, Elizabeth Shown, ed. *Professional Genealogy: A Manual for Researchers, Writers, Editors, Lecturers, and Librarians.* Baltimore: Genealogical Publishing Co., 2001.

Walking Tours

Dale, Alzina. *Mystery Reader's Walking Guide: Chicago*. Lincoln, NE: iUniverse, Inc., 2002.

Dale, Alzina. *Mystery Reader's Walking Guide: New York*. Lincoln, NE: iUniverse, Inc., 2002.

Paranormal Investigation

Hines, Terence. *Pseudoscience and the Paranormal*. Amherst, NY: Prometheus Books, 2001.

LeShan, Lawrence. *The Medium, the Mystic, and the Physicist: Toward a General Theory of the Paranormal*. New York: Allworth Press, 2003.

Writers and Literary Agents

Allen, Moira Anderson. *Writer's Guide to Queries, Pitches, and Proposals*. New York: Allworth Press, 2001.

Brogan, Kathryn S. *2004 Writer's Market*. Cincinnati: Writer's Digest Books, 2004.

Feiertag, Joe. *The Writer's Market Companion*. Cincinnati: F&W Publications, 2004.

Larsen, Michael. *How to Write a Book Proposal*, 3rd Edition. Cincinnati: F&W Publications, 2004.

Ross, Tom. *Complete Guide to Self-Publishing*, 4th Edition. Cincinnati: F&W Publications, 2002.

Books by the People Profiled in These Pages

Bernardin, Tom. *The Ellis Island Immigrant Cookbook*. New York: Tom Bernardin, Inc., 1997.

Cassell, Dana K. *Climb the Mountains to Freelance Success: Steps 1–100*. North Stratford, NH: CNW Publishing, 2002.

Cassell, Dana K., and Rose R. Noel. *The Encyclopedia of Auto-Immune Diseases*. New York: Facts on File, 2003.

Cassell, Dana K., and David H. Gleaves. *Food for Thought: The Sourcebook for Obesity and Eating Disorders*. New York: Checkmark Books, 2000.

Hirsch, David. *Moosewood Restaurant Kitchen Garden*. New York: Simon & Schuster, 1992.

Moosewood Collective. *Moosewood Restaurant Cooks at Home*. New York: Simon & Schuster, 1994.

Moosewood Collective. *Moosewood Restaurant Cooks for a Crowd*. Hoboken: John Wiley, 1996.

Moosewood Collective. *Moosewood Restaurant Low-Fat Favorites*. New York: Clarkson Potter, 1996.

Moosewood Collective. *Moosewood Restaurant's Book of Desserts*. New York: Clarkson Potter, 1997.

Moosewood Collective. *New Recipes from Moosewood Restaurant*. Berkeley: Ten Speed Press, 1987.

Moosewood Collective. *Sundays at Moosewood Restaurant*. New York: Simon & Schuster, 1990.

Nickell, Joe. *Real-Life X-Files: Investigating the Paranormal*. Lexington: University of Kentucky Press, 2001.

Nickell, Joe. *Inquest on the Shroud of Turin: Latest Scientific Findings*. New York: Prometheus Books, 1999.

Nickell, Joe. *Looking for a Miracle: Weeping Icons, Relics, Stigmata, Visions, and Healing Cures*. New York: Prometheus Books, 1999.

Nickell, Joe. *Pen, Ink, and Evidence: A Study of Writing and Writing Materials for the Penman, Collector, and Document Detective*. New Castle, DE: Oak Knoll Books, 2002.

About the Author

B lythe Camenson was a self-starter before she'd ever heard of the term. She put herself through college, then years later got on a plane bound for Saudi Arabia. She worked in various Persian Gulf countries for almost eight years. After being evacuated from Baghdad in 1990, she began a career as a freelance writer, then founded Fiction Writer's Connection, a membership organization formed to help new writers improve their craft and get published.

She is also a full-time writer of career books. Her main concern is helping job seekers make educated choices. She firmly believes that with enough information, readers can find long-term, satisfying careers. To that end, she researches traditional as well as unusual occupations, talking to a variety of professionals about what their jobs are really like. In all of her books, she includes firsthand accounts from people who can reveal what to expect in each occupation.

Camenson was educated in Boston, earning her B.A. in English and psychology from the University of Massachusetts and her M.Ed. in counseling from Northeastern University.

WESTMEATH LIBRARY
WITHDRAWN STOCK